THE SOUND OF REVELRY

This book is to be return

10. JUN

22. JUL 78

18. AUG 78

24. AUG 78
09. SEP 78

10. OCT 78
DON 21/8/78
3/12/78 S 6

18/5/79 A 6

25. AUG 79

04. SEP 79

05. DEC 79

19. JAN 80

80

10. MAY 80

24. JUL 80

02. JAN 81

13. JAN 81

07. MAR 81

The Sound of Revelry

RUPERT CROFT-COOKE

LONDON   W. H. ALLEN   1969

© RUPERT CROFT-COOKE 1969

PRINTED IN GREAT BRITAIN BY

ALDEN & MOWBRAY LTD OXFORD

FOR THE PUBLISHERS

W. H. ALLEN & CO LTD

ESSEX STREET LONDON WC2

BOUND IN LONDON BY

G & J KITCAT LTD

491 00421 4

Contents

Prefatory Note

THIS is the story of the last two years before the outbreak of the Second World War as experienced by an Englishman of military age. In it I have recalled the mounting climax through the normal, sometimes trivial events of a not very extraordinary life, and through the eyes of friends in France and Germany. I have tried to avoid those feats of hindsight by which so many historians have achieved mastery of the period for I was as baffled as most and maintained futile hopes of peace when I should have realized the inevitability of war.

But I am not concerned in this book with my own reactions except in so far as they may reveal something of the period, something that does not seem to appear in the fiction and non-fiction which I have read in an effort to know how others felt, or believed they felt, at the time.

Although this will be recognized as part of a sequence by those who know what I am attempting in this series of books, it is, more than most, an independent volume with a particular theme which I hope may be read without any knowledge of its predecessors.

It may be over ambitious to try to catch the tone of an epoch through individual experience, to say to those who did not share it: 'This is what it was like to be alive at that time.' That is what I have attempted.

CHAPTER ONE

A London Home

NINETEEN thirty-eight—looking back now with hard-earned hindsight we see the date as almost indistinguishable from those of the second World War, or at least as marking the very eve of its outbreak. In fact to those of us who lived through it as adults it seemed the twentieth year of peace rather than the precursory one of war. True we had what we optimistically called a 'war scare' as we turned back with relief to our previous occupations. But these still absorbed us.

In February of that year, nineteen months before the declaration of war and more than two years before the invasion of the Low Countries, I realized a long-nurtured ambition and moved into a flat which I had rented in London, determined that I would be 'in the heart of things', whatever I meant by that.

I had just returned from a wintry journey through ten European countries, travelling in a living-waggon with two sons of a circus family as my companions, to collect material for a book called *The Man in Europe Street*. It was time now to have done with such outlandish adventures and find the place in London life which, I believed, my authorship of a dozen novels should give me. This would turn out to be a forlorn and illusory notion for I was inhibited by temperament from any settled or respectable place in society, even literary society. But at the time it seemed—as most things seemed in my thirties—easy to achieve and quite desirable.

For Londoners and for those like me bred in the Home Counties for whom London is periodically a dwelling-place, Hyde Park is a no man's land between the familiar and the foreign. One belongs by circumstances, perhaps by character, either to the north side of the park or the south and few people find it easy to change their associations and move, say, from Bayswater to Chelsea, or from Earl's Court to St John's Wood. From the first I had belonged to the north and most of my friends with me. My first London digs were in Bryanston Street and in the '20s I had shared a flat in the dismal purlieus of Westbourne Terrace. I had lived in a negro home near Regent's Park and stayed often at Louis Golding's in Hamilton Terrace. Only twice had I shown disloyalty, once by sharing a Mews flat off Rutland Gate and once by exchanging for a few weeks my Cotswold cottage for some rooms in Oakley Street. So when I looked for a flat in 1938 I instinctively chose the north, and found what I wanted in Upper Berkeley Street which, in spite of its high-sounding name, is a turning off the Edgware Road.

But it was eight years—an enormous length of time when the years are from twenty-seven to thirty-five in one's own life —since I had lived in London at all, and I meant to remedy this provincialism. Where should a 'promising young novelist' (as I was still politely called) live but in London?

The flat was on the third (and top) floor of number 43, exactly opposite a synagogue. It was too large for me and I would share it with my friend John Hitchcock until his marriage, which was in sight. It had two sitting-rooms and two bedrooms, a very large kitchen and a very small bathroom, and it had that air of happiness, well-being, gaiety which is perceptible in some homes and cannot be created in others. In my years in the Cotswolds and Kent and in my travels I had accumulated enough old furniture and bric-à-brac to give it what is ambiguously called 'character'. It was not, I hope, 'in good taste' but it was interesting and friendly, the home of someone who treasured his finds. I had collected early English water-colours and old Italian pottery and examples of these were round me then as they are today. The books were first editions, the furniture was English of the eighteenth century. The place was fit, I felt, for the entertainment of the distin-

guished people whom no doubt I should meet and there would
be conversations on books which would continue till the
small hours.

It had its disadvantages. The bath was so small that as soon
as one got into it the water level rose to put the waste pipe in
action which flooded the flat beneath and brought harassed
neighbours to the door complaining that their curtains were
ruined. The landlords, Bovis, wrote me harsh letters on the
subject but I pointed out that their only remedy was to put in
a larger bath. It took no Archimedes, I told them, to see that
the displacement caused by a human body raised the water level.

The rent (water and rates included) was £3 a week and it
will seem curious to a younger generation of home-seekers in
London that I had the choice of half a dozen flats at similar
prices in that immediate district though the postal address was
W.1—a consideration at that time.

If my plans for this to be a centre of culture and polite
conversation were serious (and I cannot believe I knew myself
so little), they were soon destroyed. I found that area of
London, Speakers' Corner and the Edgware Road, rich in
noctambules, down-and-out and sometimes desperate men,
strange outer-fringe characters to be met in bars and during
the small hours in milk-bars, and the conversation in my low-
ceilinged room was anything but literary or cultured. I delighted in the variety of these and what Wilde had once called
their infamous war against life. I gathered a highly miscellaneous circle of aquaintance and felt myself with it in spirit as
I had been in rural England and abroad, knowing that this was
inconsistent with any sort of social ambition. I could not, as
Louis Golding did, keep my friends in compartments and I
lived from day to day among them in great contentment.

When I needed a secretary I took on, at a miserable salary,
a young Communist named Richard Parker whom I had met
by chance in Maidstone. He was full of idealism but it was
salted with a mature and good-humoured cynicism about me,
my work and most other things. He accepted wholeheartedly

the discipline of the Party and in theory at least was hostile to my way of life and scornful of my natural anarchism. But he worked for me loyally enough, perhaps because he could find no other employment in London and wanted to be near his girl friend. I was conscious that behind his reserve he had ardent enthusiasms, for Communism, for Indian Nationalism, for the poetry of Spender and Auden, and given the power would have been quite ruthless with the fuddy-duddy bourgeois world he believed me to represent. But I liked his ironical manner and his sincerity and realized that he acted as some curb on my expansive egotism.

Some, but not much. For there I was at the beginning of 1938, feeling that the world was mine, seeing my own career as rising to fulfilment, believing my novels to be far, far better than they were and my reputation as a writer a good deal higher than it was—or ever would be. I was my own master, earning enough to live as I wanted, to have this pleasant flat, my yellow Alsatian Dingo, my middle-aged Lanchester car which gave me a sense of freedom. I could travel abroad fairly often and still felt the world was my oyster. I did not have to remember that I was perpetually in debt, that the car had not been paid for and the whole set-up depended on my health and ability to write another book. I do not think I was arrogant or vain, but I was openly pleased with myself and with what I believed to be my achievements, perhaps a little surprised that no one, and least of all Richard Parker, seemed to envy them. But I was fortunately too energetic and happy for complacency.

I must have been in some ways ridiculous. I affected cosmopolitanism, wearing an immense fur-coat, purchased in the Telekitér at Budapest, and other noticeable foreign clothes. I was usually surrounded by young friends and inclined to be scornful of less exhibitionistic people and their good citizenship. I belonged to no club, no clique, no party and felt no need of the support, professional or social, derived from fellowship with other rebellious characters. I could behave myself by conventional standards when I chose and wear a pinstripe suit

when the occasion demanded, because I was *au fond* a gregarious creature and had inherited, if I had not retained, the
middle-class standards of my parents. But I suppose I saw
myself as beyond these, in a delightful world of my own creation.

I was proud, above all else, of being a professional writer
and saw everything that happened to me, every journey I made,
every new encounter, as grist to the literary mill. I read very
little and was uncomprehending of the literary and political
movements of the time and vociferously contemptuous of
most of them. 'For to admire an' for to see, For to be'old this
world so wide . . .' I thought of Rudyard Kipling who had
given me my first encouragement when he had asked me to
his home sixteen years earlier, and I saw him and Joseph
Conrad as the two modern writers I admired most because they
had turned red-blooded experience into literature. All this
would have been understandable in a youth in his twenties,
but I was thirty-five and really should have learned to think
and behave as an adult.

The influence of what my father called 'a good woman'
would certainly have brought me to discretion, but the women
who were my friends at this time would not have been
generally described as good, and I had missed the encouragement of a wife who wanted her husband to be like other hus-
bands, only better. So it always surprised me when I was
treated as an established author with an entry in *Who's Who*
and an overdraft. I expected people, solid grown-up people
like bank managers and publishers, to see through my bluff
and know that they were dealing with a secretly timid adolescent masquerading as a man of the world.

[2]

Yet the household was not a disorderly one even if it was
visited by incongruous people. John went off to his office

punctually in the morning after our large and plethoric char, Mrs Judge, had given us breakfast. At thirty shillings a week for six hours' work a day there were plenty of kindly women to look after bachelors in those years, regarding their earnings as pocket-money, their labour as not intolerably onerous, and their time spent in someone else's home a change from the somewhat dreary conditions in their own. This was the third stage in the emancipation of domestic servants from the scandalous slavery of Victorian times when unfortunate girls in basements and attics were underpaid and underfed, down to the present when their equally unfortunate employers are cheated of ten shillings an hour and a substantial meal for a little token duster-flicking. Between these came the Edwardian era when householders commiserated with one another on the servant problem ('So hard to get!' 'So independent!'), but supplied caps and aprons for afternoon wear, and the period between the wars when equity and give-and-take on both sides were the general rule.

Mrs Judge was not 'a treasure' but she 'managed very well' and by her sage and sober manner gave a settled air to my home.

After John's departure for the office Richard Parker would arrive and sit down before the typewriter to read the *Daily Worker* while in the next room I must have done some writing. But I had no routine. Throughout that year and the next I wrote only sporadically or while staying abroad, and every day saw incidents, encounters, diversions which left no time or energy for solid work. Sometimes I cooked lunch, at others ate veal scallops, or in impecunious periods spaghetti at the Italian café-restaurant across the road.

[3]

During my first months in the flat I saw nothing of the Rosaires for their circus had started its tenting season and was

lost somewhere in the English countryside. I have described
this remarkable family in *The Happy Highways* and need say here
only that it consisted of the Count and Countess (they followed
the circus custom of adopting titles, like Lord John Sanger and
Sir Robert Fossett), their four sons Aubrey, Dennis, Ivor and
Derrick, and their four daughters Cissie, Zena, Vivienne and
Ida, who with a few supernumeraries, some tent-men, a clown,
a 'little fellow' and the owner of two performing elephants
provided the whole programme of a sizable tenting show.
I had travelled with them for a few weeks in the previous year
and Ivor and Derrick had been with me as far as Czechoslovakia and Hungary on my *Man in Europe Street* trip. While
we had been away the Count had taken charge of Dingo, my
yellow Alsatian, and it was to recover that magnificent creature,
my closest companion for five years, that I set out to find the
circus now.

But this was not easy. As protection against their competi-
tors, circuses were secretive about their routes and there was
no general post office for them. I bought the *World's Fair*, the
weekly newspaper of the circus and fair ground, in the hope
that there might be some reference to the Rosaires which
would serve as a guide. By luck there was a paragraph con-
gratulating them on effective billposting in St Neots on the
previous Thursday. 'St Neots,' I read in the A.A. book,
'Hunts. London 56½ miles.' Well, that would have to serve.
Accompanied by Louis Golding I set off on a cold Saturday
afternoon to find them some ten days after they had left
St Neots, knowing only that I must start from there.

In St Neots itself there were evidences still of the effective
billposting which had impressed the *World's Fair*, but it gave
no indication of the direction they had taken. The police,
however, believed that they had gone towards Kimbolton.
At Kimbolton an old man remembered that there had been a
circus in the town last week, but he had not seen it himself.
Passers-by, called in for information, agreed that it had gone
to Brampton. At Brampton the bills were a little fresher, and

at Alconbury a garage man had seen the show and thought it good. It had left there, he said, for Thrapston.

I was now close on its heels, but it was beginning to grow dusk before I saw suddenly, in the very centre of the road, undisturbed by traffic or road-sweepers, the unmistakable shape of elephant droppings.

I pointed these out to Louis and told him their significance. Only Salt and Saucy, the Rosaires' elephants, could have been responsible and we must be close behind them. This delighted Louis who had a lively sense of oddity.

"Elephant droppings," he repeated ecstatically and afterwards wrote a short story on the theme.

It was almost dusk when we ran them to earth at Corby in Northamptonshire.

There was something extraneous about this background for their tent and coloured waggons which I had always seen in rustic surroundings.

The town itself was not large, but on its outskirts had been constructed the vast iron-smelting plant of Stewarts & Lloyds, a monstrous white smoke-belching anomaly in that pleasant countryside. Against the darkening sky its furnaces were red and lurid, and the *tober* itself unusually obscure, except for the lighted front of the big tent. We had little time—only enough to collect Dingo, have a cup of tea in the Countess's waggon, go round and greet everybody, swallow a glass of beer with the Count in a crowded pub, and leave them starting the evening show. Their waggons and lorries, their tents and horses, seemed flimsy with the ironworks behind them, but they themselves, playing to an audience of iron-workers, living in their small movable homes, were serene and independent. The forces of industry, which to me seem always monstrous, had no meaning for them. There are no bosses and unions and labour troubles in the circus, and the belching chimneys which lit the sky about them were happily uninteresting to them. Corby was a place at which they were showing—nothing more.

[4]

Dingo had never lived in a city and gave embarrassing proof of it on the pavements of the Edgware Road, but he was a blissfully unselfish dog, never demanding anything for his own comfort or pleasure, patiently waiting for his food or for a walk in the park. He returned at once to his habit of following me from room to room, even from chair to chair, and his personal beauty gave lustre to the carpets he lay on.

But he detested small boys, particularly when they rushed about in a mob, shoving and ragging one another. Coming home from Hyde Park one afternoon he found himself behind a group of these just outside my flat, and picked out one particularly noisy and active. This was, moreover, like Grainger in Oscar Wilde's fatal words 'a peculiarly plain boy—unfortunately extremely ugly'. Dingo suddenly went forward and nipped him shrewdly in the bottom.

At first the boy scarcely noticed it. He gave a brief 'Ough' and his hand went down, for he thought one of his friends had pinched him. But when he turned round and saw Dingo he did a double-take and set up a howling which brought passers-by to a standstill. A friendly barber standing in the door of his shop saw what had happened and took him inside for an application of iodine though the skin was unbroken and only two red marks showed on the surface. Then the police arrived.

The London police still retained, in those days, their traditional calm and ability to cope with unusual street incidents without self-importance or bluster. The assertive and insolent bully quite common today was unknown and they seemed to regard the public out of uniform as so many helpless foreigners whom they were employed to assist. The young man who spoke to me made no comment but took my name and address and said that as a police car was handy they would send the boy home in it. "That'll cheer him up," he added. "He's had a bit of a turn, I expect."

That evening an aggressive father arrived at the flat and asked bluntly for compensation. I told him that I was insured against any harm the dog might do and suggested that if he had any claim to make he should put it on paper. This infuriated him and he demanded that I there and then give him the sum of £3 10s. which ought, he said, to be at least a fiver because his son was suffering from a nasty shock.

A tiresome argument ensued in which I stuck to my insurance policy—a useful document which covered one against all third-party risks apart from motoring and cost 5s. a year—and he lowered his claim to £3. "And that", I told him in the words of Mr Pecksniff to Montague Tigg, "is equally impossible." He grew threatening and said, "You may not be aware of it but in these cases the police may order the dog to be destroyed." "In this case," I said more offensively, "they are more likely to order the boy to be destroyed." On that he said I should 'hear more of this' and walked out.

[5]

A livelier confrontation took place a few weeks later. I am not proud of my irresponsibility or my living on a shoestring with unpaid bills accumulating, nor do I seek to justify it by claiming that as a writer I was underpaid, for I was as conscious as ever of the miracle of being paid at all for doing what I liked to do. But I can see now how this led to warfare, usually good-humoured, with my creditors, not to avoid payment but to counter their demands for money when I had not got it. A cynic might say this came to the same thing, but I did not intend it to and like most people who lived in the red in those lean years, never contracted a debt which I did not intend to settle.

The typewriter, for instance, which I was buying by in-stalments, caused me and Richard Parker some anxious moments. Payments were in arrears, to the number of three I seem to remember, and one afternoon when I was out a character arrived with an order to seize it.

Now this man I took to be that personal enemy of all improvident people—a debt-collector. He might be an impeccable citizen, a good husband and father, but he had come, I rather dramatically said, to deprive me of my means of livelihood and right or wrong it was my plain duty to outwit him. Some money had arrived that morning and I sent Richard to pay up arrears, *not* to the debt-collecting agency but to the shop from whom we purchased the thing. They accepted it cheerfully and gave us a receipt.

In my school history book there was a picture of two stern-faced men in billycock hats seizing a sewing-machine from an undernourished widow with a handkerchief to her eyes. This was not the scene in my flat next morning, but it might have resembled it if we had not taken precautions.

I supposed the receipt from the shop would settle the matter, but not at all. The money should have been paid through the debt-collector who would now miss his commission on it. He made it plain in a loud voice as he stood outside the front door that he had an order to seize the typewriter and meant to do so. "And don't say it's not here," he said, "because I *heard* it!"

He was just what one imagined a bumbailiff to be like— large, pompous, black-clad and hectoring. Perhaps he imagined that I should be embarrassed by other flat-holders over-hearing him.

Refused admission he stamped away to fetch a policeman. He knew his rights, he said, a claim which I have learned in the years since that spring morning to be one of the most idiotic, in any circumstances, to pass the lips of man. He returned with a large ginger-haired policeman who explained the law to us all solemnly.

"This man," he said, "has an order to seize your typewriter. He is therefore entitled to entry to effect that purpose."

They both thereupon came in.

"On the other hand he has not a search warrant so he is not entitled to disturb the contents of the flat in any way or otherwise inconvenience the occupants."

With that he marched off to his duties, leaving the debt-collector seated in Richard's room.

"You might as well hand it over," he said. "Because I'm not leaving here till I've got it."

Impasse.

After ten minutes I asked him to leave.

"I'm not leaving till I have that typewriter, and you can't make me."

Growing exasperated I told Richard to find the ginger-haired policeman and bring him back. This Solomon in uniform duly appeared and made his pronouncement.

"I cannot eject this man from your flat," he said. "But you are entitled to eject him in certain conditions. You may only use what force is necessary to remove him from the premises and if a disturbance is caused by your action I should have to intervene. On the other hand, if a disturbance is caused by unnecessary resistance on his part I can take him in charge for causing . . . " Did he say 'an affray'? I can scarcely suppose so, but it was some quasi-legal term which seemed to impress the debt-collector.

"I shouldn't be suprised if it was in that chest," he said, watching our faces.

It was not. It was under my bed in the next room.

His manner suddenly changed and grew quiet and bitter.

"Oh well. There you are. Can't waste any more time. I suppose you think you've been very clever. You wait till the next time you run into arrears. You won't know I'm coming, then."

He made for the door and the ginger-haired policeman followed him, pausing to voice a summarizing reflection.

"We've all got to earn a living somehow," he said and with a suggestion of a smile walked out.

[6]

But the police, in plain clothes, were back in the flat some weeks later, this time to investigate an attempted robbery.

Nothing shows the change in economic conditions since that date more clearly than the rise in value of the prizes for which men will risk their liberty. Nowadays a professional thief thinks a thousand nicker a poor reward for a night's screwing and will not go out for less, whereas then there were plenty of marauders satisfied with a few chancy pounds. The penalties for offences against property, which might after all have been the judge's property, were as disproportionately heavy compared with penalties for all other crimes then as today, and for large-scale swindlers like Hatry and his associates far heavier. It would have caused no suprise between the wars, as it did in the case of the train robbers thirty years later, if those unable to buy their freedom were given twenty years apiece (or twice the average time actually served by offenders doing life sentence for murder) for a spectacular robbery almost without violence. Petty theft and impromptu housebreaking were rampant and often escaped detection.

I returned to the flat one afternoon to find the front door forced open by a jemmy, a number of letters pushed through the letter-box and lying on the floor and nothing whatever missing. I telephoned for the police and a loquacious and amused plain clothes man called an hour later and took the situation in at a glance.

"It's the classic method," he said over a cup of tea. "The postman disturbed him. Tell you how it's done. Two men work together. They find a block of flats like this one, not too large and no hall-porter. One stands in the entrance downstairs while the other goes to the top floor and rings a doorbell. If you had been in and replied he would have pretended to sell you something and gone away when you refused. But if there's no reply he forces the door and does a quick go-over of the contents. He'll only be disturbed probably if any one enters the building from the street and his mate's there to warn him of that with a whistle. There's a chance in a thousand that someone might come out of another flat on the same floor at the very moment he's breaking in, but even then he'll be out and away before anything can be done about it. He can't go wrong, can he?"

I was impressed by his knowledge and asked why nothing had been taken.

"Obvious, isn't it? The postman walked in downstairs just as he forced the door and he got the signal to blow. Or else there was nothing handy. Jewellery and money's what they chiefly go for."

I asked if this kind of larceny was common.

"Course it is. There's dozens of them working at it. If we pick up one pair another takes over."

This gave me a picture of two-man teams industriously at work daily all over the metropolitan area.

"But there's not many places as handy for them as this. Just three floors and a nice quiet building. Couldn't be handier."

Could nothing be done about it I asked.

"What can be done? Let me ask *you* that. You tell me. How would you go about stopping it?"

"I should have thought those engaged in it might be identified and watched."

The detective smiled and shook his head.

"Far too many of them and too few of us," he said blandly. "Now'n again we're lucky; more often they are."

"So this may happen again?"

The detective was beaming now.

"Shouldn't think so. Lightning doesn't strike in the same place twice, does it?"

[7]

Incident was what attracted me, in life as in fiction, particularly incident which provided scope for bar-side narrative in which the oddity and uncertainty of life could be treated as comedy. London gave me this and much else and I woke each day with delight to the knowledge that I was in London, was at least temporarily a Londoner.

So much so that for a long time the world beyond had very little significance for me except perhaps the events of the Spanish Civil War which in that spring were heartrending to anyone who loved Spain as I did yet could not see a clean-cut issue or ally himself wholeheartedly with one side or the other. The war was at its most agonizing with both forces still hopeful of victory though the Nationalists were advancing into Catalonia. The Italians were merrily bombing Barcelona from the Balearic Islands though all three, the Italian Command, Franco's High Command and the Italian High Command in Italy, disclaimed responsibility for these raids. (Why was not the local commander arrested after World War II and judged as a war criminal? A dangerous precedent, perhaps, to consider those who ordered raids involving civilian deaths as war criminals. Yet why not, if he acted on his own initiative?) These raids did as much as anything to stir indignation in England and there were meetings everywhere addressed by furious speakers, and young men volunteered in great numbers to join the Republican Army. Everywhere I saw slogans— *Arms for Spain, Stop the War, Up the Republic, Down with Franco,* but non-intervention was proved to be a farce and when in April Chamberlain recognized Mussolini's conquest of Ethiopia and thus tacitly his intervention in Spain, Eden resigned, but *politics* went on their craven course unchanged. Hitler had grabbed Austria a month earlier and in France Blum failed to revive the Popular Front. It was a very mad world that spring, and any fool, one might think, could see that a world war was imminent.

But it was not quite as easy as that. Hindsight is a most attractive palliative for our own humiliating lack of judgment. It is so easy to see now that each of us should have been preparing himself for what was inevitable, but we forget that each had his personal affairs, his ambitions and concern with the enormous urgencies of every day. Our attitudes to war were various, but almost equally blind. "Well, if it comes, it comes." Or, "Better have it and get it over with". Or, "Hitler will never dare to go to war. Did you hear about those cardboard tanks?" Meanwhile my friends in Germany, no more percipient, were repeating: "Hitler has said he only wants areas of predominantly German population." Or, "He is a man of peace. Why would he be raising all these fine buildings if he means to involve us in war?" Each had his own kind of wishful thinking and mine, for a long time, was not to think at all on world issues.

CHAPTER TWO

The Brown Tower

LET me turn for relief, though not altogether comic, to the person and personality of my friend Louis Golding. I saw much of him during those two years before the war, and for most part with pleasure, though a certain change in our relationship was already perceptible, presaging the sorrier days ahead. I was no longer prepared to listen with quite so much attention when he lectured me on the commercial aspect of writing, was beginning to doubt whether he was after all a master of it. His tireless haggling over guineas and half-guineas with busy editors in accordance with his belief that any fee offered to him could be increased, might not, I began to think, be as shrewd as it had seemed. The truth was that from being a quirk which amused his friends, Louis's cupidity and avarice were becoming an obsession and over-shadowed much that was likable in the man. There were ways in which he was generous; he would devote time and go to some trouble in giving advice which he knew was helpful. In fact that avarice and that cupidity were almost extraneous to his nature as a whole, a kind of insanity, but one could not always remember or sympathize with that.

Nor, in the later years, was it easy to be invariably good-natured and amused about Louis's overwhelming vanity and self-deception, and make anecdotes of them as one can today. There were times when I at least was exasperated into blunt-ness. Against this he was almost impregnable, and if by chance I thrust between the armour I was always sorry for it. He was not easily hurt, but pain when he felt it was in the depths of his being, down among the complexes.

Yet he was never a bore. He was of course highly intelligent, often witty and only in regard to himself without a sense of humour. He talked well and he made others talk. With a little admiration to encourage him he lit up and gave more than we who listened had given by that impetus. I counted myself lucky in his aquaintance and knew that however much at times I detested his shameless parsimony and the illusions of grandeur with which he surrounded himself, he influenced and enriched my life.

He was now in his middle forties, a plump vivacious man with a mind almost too agile, and a rich cultivated voice. Intensely realistic in many things, as a writer he lived in a dream world built from early longings and ambitions and from tales of other writers in Edwardian times. In the period at which his writing career began there was a well-defined line of progress for the successful, first encouragement and head-patting from the great, then public recognition and increasing prosperity, then fame, wealth, and a magnificent home like Abbotsford, Farringdon, Bateman's, a title perhaps or at least an Order of Merit. Louis had achieved so much against such odds that he felt cheated of the rewards. Eight years earlier he had published his best-selling novel *Magnolia Street* and he could never understand, bless him, why it did not earn him a place at the very peak of the contemporary Olympus, and why he had to say of himself the things he wanted to hear from others.

His house in Hamilton Terrace was all he had as fulfilment of his hopes and ambitions in the striving and homeless years that had preceded *Magnolia Street* (or *Maggy* as he called that novel, insisting that his friends should use the term). It was furnished with rococo exaggeration, pink and naked carved figures of the Child Jesus which he had purchased in Spain during the church-looting days of the Republic were clustered round the walls and among them Louis, another round fat

cherub though not as free from malice, moved about talking
vigorously and offering, on rare occasions and sparingly, a
glass of sherry to select guests.

If the hospitality he provided in his own house lacked pro-
digality, his demands from anyone rash enough to invite him
to another home, even for a party, were lavish. In the first
place it had to be made plain, with exuberant tact, that his
host or hostess should realize the distinction he was conferring
by his presence.

"Oh, Florence," I would hear him on the phone. "About
your dinner-party on Thursday. You know I'm working
immensely hard just now and really ought not to go out at all.
I feel that when I *do* make an exception I am bound by my own
conscience to be sure that it will give me real relaxation. I'm
sure you understand? No, no. It's not that. I'm sure you will.
Only I do seem to remember that last time I came to you there
was some confusion about places at the table and I found myself
next to rather . . . Oh, of course! On your right? That will be
. . . You are always so gracious. I was going to ask you if I
might bring my friend Charles Smith . . . Yes. A naval
officer. In civvies of course. I'm afraid he hasn't a dinner-
jacket in London. But of course you understand."

How much his hostess understood I could never decide, but
she certainly did not guess that Charlie Smith was a naval
rating whom Louis had picked up in a pub a few days earlier.

"Yes I knew you would. That is most charming of you. Of
course Stanley is going to pick us up in the car as he so
very kindly did last time? He can't? Oh, but . . . You see, I
really counted on that when I accepted . . . I know, but I have
to work that day till the very last moment. Surely the car will
be repaired by then? You see, it means so *much* to me if
someone . . . That is *most* kind of you. You know how I
appreciate it."

I would be full of admiration. Louis regarded the payment
of taxi fares as the worst kind of extravagance and showed
immense ingenuity in avoiding it, even when he had ridden

with others. With diabolical skill, speed and accuracy he could divide the total of a fare and tip between three or four people and produce his share as the taxi drew to the kerb. If he could not, with some resourceful argument, persuade his hosts to send or call for him he would ask me, or some other friend with a car, to drive him over.

"They will be delighted if you come," he used to tell me, but experience had made me cagey of joining him however persuasive he became. A hurt, resentful manner, familiar to all his friends, would appear when he failed to get his own way, and though it would seem that he had changed the subject of conversation, as an expert Louisian I would know that he was only attacking from another angle.

"You really *should* widen your acquaintance, Rupert. I feel that, even in reading your books. You tend to present the types you meet in pubs. You have so many chances with me of coming to know interesting people. I can't understand why you don't take advantage of them."

When no transport was available or when an invitation promised nothing but old friends or people of no interest to Louis, he would refuse it, especially when he was coming to the end of a book.

"If I were to go I should only start being brilliant and then be too exhausted to work tomorrow," he once told me as he put down the phone after a wordy refusal. He had wanted *me* to say that, and I knew it. Why could I so rarely bring out the words which would give him so much pleasure? I was not a mean man with praise. But Louis made it difficult for one to say the things he longed to hear. He was so very palpable.

[2]

He accepted several invitations from me during those two years though he was not always happy in the result. There was an occasion when he was in the flat one afternoon at the same time as a number of young writers who, as I shall recount, had some business with me. Richard Parker had just published his first short story, Ruthven Todd was there and a brilliant young man named John Mair who had written a book on the Ireland Shakespeare forgeries.

Louis instinctively took the chair.

"As writers yourselves," he told my astonished friends, "you will be interested in what I am going to ask you. I am confronted with the problem of a title. This is something you will all have to face in the future and I should like to see if any of you has any suggestion to make."

I felt the most acute mortification on his behalf. Couldn't he see that they were all concerned with their own literary affairs, that they knew him only as the author of a best-selling novel which they had not read, that they could not care less about him, or his new book, or its title? But Louis truly believed that the occasion would be memorable to them in the future as his own first meeting with Israel Zangwill had been memorable to him. He saw himself as a Great Man being encouraging and not too patronizing to the young. He believed that they felt themselves privileged.

He went on to expound the plot of the book which appeared later as *Mr Emmanuel*, the story of an obscure Jewish business-man who becomes a hero by venturing into Nazi Germany.

"I thought of using the line from *Lear, Child Roland to the Dark Tower came* . . ."

"Browning used that," said John Mair suppressing a yawn.

"Of course, but I want only the allusion. I meant to suggest the grim fortress of the Brownshirts. I thought perhaps *The Brown Tower*."

"How now, brown cow," someone said—I feel sure it was Ruthven Todd.

Louis had such reverence for youth that he managed an uncomfortable smile.

"Yes, it does sound rather like that, doesn't it?" he said and the subject of his title was dropped.

Afterwards he lectured me severely.

"You seem to meet altogether the wrong sort of young writers," he said.

But that was not the worst thing that happened to him in my flat. In the following year, after John was married, when my co-tenant was a man named Myles Eadon, Louis came to a party at which the guests were friends of mine, chiefly writers, or friends of Myles, chiefly lovely young women in gay summer frocks. He had been warned that it would not be the kind of party he was likely to enjoy but he had smiled at the idea of any party of which he would not be the centre. When he found that he was treated with polite lack of recognition he sulked.

There was a young novelist named Nina Warner Hooke who had written a trilogy about which I was enthusiastic. I called her to my aid.

"That's Louis Golding over there in the corner. Be an angel and go and tell him you think he's our greatest living novelist. It will cheer him up a lot."

Nina astounded me.

"Of course," she said. "Besides, I *do* think so. Or very nearly."

She approached Louis.

"Mr Golding," she said. "You are looking at your greatest fan."

Louis beamed and Nina sat at his knee.

"And which of my novels did you like best?" asked Louis.

Nina seemed to consider this deeply.

"I think probably *The Rains Came*," she said. She was quite sincere but never could remember names. Louis left the party.

[3]

Every summer Louis used to spend a couple of weeks at a boys' holiday camp. He had been telling me about this for years. 'Enchanting' was the word he used when he tried to persuade me to join him, and I could never make him see that a mob of snotty-nosed small boys had no enchantment for me.

"You can have no conception," Louis said, "of the strange idyllic quality of it. The youngsters are from a school for orphans and to see them respond to the sea, and the open air, feeling they are some concern to older people, is the most richly rewarding thing I have known."

He believed it. He believed it was to watch them responding to the open air that he went every year, nominally as an adult 'helper' at the camp, in fact as a middle-aged man revitalizing himself in young boys' company with pederastic undertones. (I use the word pederast to mean what the Greeks meant by it, so far as the little Greek I remember serves me—a lover of boys, specifically, even of small boys. It should not be confused as it was by certain ill-informed old gentlemen in the House of Lords at the time of the Wolfenden Report debates with 'homosexual', a bastard word in any case.) Louis was not a pederast in any sense which would have brought him into conflict with the laws protecting children, and his enthusiasm for this camp seemed to me out of character. He usually detested as heartily as I did those lovesick wooers of pubescent males who are found in organizations for boys, curates, scout masters and such, votaries of the immature who idolize other people's children before their characters are formed. My own dislike of these had been based on no more than fastidiousness when I was a young man, but with time it had grown to something a good deal stronger and almost the only form of sexual morality I recognize is this—that interference with the young, or with anyone not fully in control of his or her behaviour, is culpable, even criminally culpable.

So I was prejudiced against the cause of Louis's 'enchantment' before I examined it. I must have suspected what I should be in for since I persuaded Richard Parker, on whose young cynicism I could depend, to accompany me. He was surely the most inappropriate person to visit a boys' camp and not at all pleased at leaving the company of his girl friend even for a couple of nights.

We found it quite nauseating. A conscientious high-church clergyman, the vicar of a London parish, raised the money every year from his parishioners and from 'helpers' like Louis, to take a hundred youngsters to a camp by the sea. Father Hutch, as he was known, was a heavy crop-haired sunburnt man who looked, as Richard Parker said, like Largo Caballero. He had gathered round him a group of men who were 'good with boys' (in a somewhat ambiguous phrase) to whom this fortnight in their company was an annual paradise. The boys, poor little devils, had no one to turn to but these, their elders, and gave them the artless hero-worship which young animals naturally give to beings wiser and more understanding than themselves.

It was not lecherous, but it was emotional. Father Hutch was idealistic and naturally trusted his helpers to behave themselves, but the assignations, intrigues, jealousies among both boys and helpers were endless.

I arrived with Richard late at night at the camp and we were taken to an empty tent by one of the helpers.

"I hope you will be all right in here," he giggled before leaving us.

At breakfast the 'helpers' sat in the Officers' Mess at a long table with Father Hutch at the head of it. They waited on one another, for it was a rule of the camp that the boys, whose holiday it was, should not actually wait on the men though they washed up after them. Conversation was devoted entirely to the charms of boyhood.

"D'you know what little Peter said to me last night?"

"Some of the wilder ones were taking the micky out of So-and-So yesterday. You should have seen his face!"

"What a delightful boy that young Billy is. Handsome youngster, too."

In Louis's tent after breakfast we learned of the day's programme. But when I said we wanted to swim Louis said, "Do you mind waiting till they've tidied their tents? We'll all go down to the beach together."

I soon saw the force of this. As they became free from daily duties half a dozen youngsters gathered round Louis's tent, he being their chosen adult. It was a daily occasion.

"Can I carry your camera, Mr Golding?"

"Can I take your rug?"

"I'm going to bring his book and sun-glasses, anyway," announced a third.

"Let me take the cushions."

"Isn't it divine?" asked Louis, appealing to us, and he proceeded to put on a floppy hat and march towards the sea on his little fat legs, followed by a tail of small boys, carrying his beach gear.

'Will someone kindly lead me to a pub' I quoted to Richard Parker, and after a swim we spent most of the day in the local.

Louis was never mildly peeved when I showed myself out of sympathy; he was furious. He walked about all day with an expression of frustrated anger and pain and next morning before I left he settled down to a first-class row with me. I failed to appreciate the subtlety, the delicacy, the captivating naivety of small boys. I was coarse-grained and intolerant. I might at least have shown more consideration for him.

I prepared to answer this. If it was to be a slanging match he should have it outright.

"I don't know how you, with a sense of humour, can make yourself so ridiculous," I should say. "It may be all right for homosexual parsons with arrested development and their emasculated helpers, but you're an intelligent adult, for God's sake. I think the whole thing's disgusting, so don't start talking to me about subtlety and idylls." It was not often that I made this kind of retort to Louis, but someone *had* to tell him some-times.

I was about to let fly in those terms when I saw Louis's face. "I know exactly what you're going to say," he told me, and I believe it was true. "Only don't say it, there's a good chap. You must understand that this camp means a very great deal in my life. More than you can understand."

Not more than I could understand, for the whole secret was suddenly revealed to me. It did mean a great deal in his life. This was not pederasty in any ordinary sense. These youngsters, changing from year to year, stood for all that Louis had never had, all that his singular nature had deprived him of. Baulked of his natural joy in parenthood he found some vicarious compensation here. The philoprogenitive instinct, one of the strongest and noblest qualities of his race, was somehow assuaged by these surroundings and he was able to idealize them till the shoddiness was not seen by him.

[4]

There was a sadder occasion in which Louis collaborated that year or the next, painful even to remember. Some South London borough, Battersea I think, but it may have been Brixton, had decided to stage a 'Festival of Youth', whatever that might be, and Louis had sold them the idea of employing him to write incidental words. For this he was to receive a large fee and certain privileges, free entry and association with the performers, and to make the choice of his own speaker for the Prologue he had written.

Louis set to work in all earnestness and produced some couplets which opened

> *This is a Festival of Youth*
> *Which we do here present to you . . .*

He then advertised for a suitable young man, a simple cockney proletarian who would speak his words with the right intonation. Unfortunately the young men who answered were would-be actors, would-be broadcasters, would-be's in fact of every kind, and the one he actually chose was far too genteel for the occasion and spoke his lines as though he had just come from an elocution lesson. Moreover, he insisted on wearing a dinner-jacket. He had, it seemed, ambitions which Louis encouraged, somewhat at the expense of the Festival of Youth which was intended to be the sort of thing the young people of a Russian industrial town might offer to Stalin on his birthday.

The Festival of Youth opened in a torrent of rain, and rain continued to fall throughout its run. Of the eight thousand people expected nightly a bare eighty sat under umbrellas and watched some heroic gymnastics and folk-dancing in a structure like a bandstand.

> *This is a Festival of Youth*
> *Which we do here present to you . . .*

read Louis's protégé every evening in his buffed-up voice, while Louis's name appeared prominently on the programme. The losses on the project were very large by the standard of that time and for some weeks Louis wrestled with his conscience about his fee, but his conscience won and he insisted on the whole of it. Only after a number of telephonic arguments did he agree to reduce it by fifteen per cent in view of the disastrous weather.

Perhaps his greatest gift was his power of persuasion. If anyone had called him glib he would have been indignant, yet in business affairs and in his books themselves that is exactly what he was—a glib writer and a glib man. He could persuade me into almost anything. When his book *In the Steps of Moses the Conqueror* appeared that summer it was sent to me by *The British Weekly** for a review. I saw its bulk and telephoned Louis with some of his own guile.

---

*A darlin' paper, as an Irish author once told me. It was in those days the voice of broadminded Noncomformity and Liberalism, and had staunch but tolerant literary values.

"You see," I explained, "I can't get down to reading it properly for a week or two. I wondered which you would prefer, a quick review to help give it a push *now*, or a more thoughtful review when I've had time to read it."

"I think that *in loyalty to my publishers* I should say that the review should appear as soon as possible."

"All right. I'll do something at once. Is there anything you particularly want brought out?"

I might have known that Louis would have a surprising reply but I was quite staggered when it came.

"What I was rather hoping *someone* would say," he answered confidentially, "was that these two books of mine* should be considered not so much as modern travel books but in the category of those great classics of the desert, *The Seven Pillars of Wisdom, Arabia Deserta, Eothen* and *The Letters of Gertrude Bell*."

"Do you really want me to say that, Louis?"

"Oh my dear old chap, I don't want you to say anything you don't feel. I was simply saying that I hoped someone would see this point."

"Very well, I'll say that," I told Louis recklessly and there it is, in the *British Weekly* of July 28, 1938, "I believe that the two books must be considered, not in the category of modern travel books, but with those classics of the desert, 'The Seven Pillars of Wisdom', 'Arabia Deserta', 'Eothen', and the 'Letters of Gertrude Bell'." How much a liar I am I do not know, for I have not read the Moses books to this day.

*In the Steps of Moses the Lawgiver, 1937, In the Steps of Moses the Conqueror, 1938.

CHAPTER THREE

To the Circus

THE dominant interest of most writers of my generation in
those years immediately before the war was political. I gave
myself to extraneous escapist things and foremost among them
was the circus. Or, more accurately, one circus, that of my
friends the Rosaires, which I had seen grow from a small
family affair to one of the largest circuses tenting that
summer.

It was not primarily a literary interest. I supposed vaguely
that I should one day write a book about the Rosaires and
thought of my travels with them as precious experience, but
I did not subscribe to the tendency made fashionable by Lady
Eleanor Smith and Dame Laura Knight to regard circus people
as colourful and exotic copy. I never became what was called
a circus fan, nor belonged to a self-conscious organization
called the Circus Fans Association and although in that winter
I went to other circuses in London, Bertram Mills's and Tom
Arnold's, I was not so much interested in the history or tradition
or mythology of the circus, as in the brave and beautiful
members of this family.

Being with them and hearing their stories of their early
beginnings meant entering two very strangely populated and
radiant worlds, both of which have now been swept away. Or
was it one world in two periods? For I saw the nomadic life
of the years between the wars, motorized, electric-lit, a little
brash and publicity-minded, but also, in the stories I heard, the
improvident wilder life of the showman driving his traction
engine or ponies through rural England in late Victorian or

Edwardian times. Both are worth preserving in memory and have escaped most social historians.

Of the first of these, the nomadic life I briefly shared, I wrote in *The Circus Has No Home* (1941) in that high-flown prose I find so irritating today but which then seemed to me fine writing:

> Moving on with them from place to place, living in a trailer-caravan, not asking the route for next week but following without a map wherever they were going from day to day, relieved one of all the business of life, letter-writing, engagement-keeping, thought for the morrow. Each day was an episode, a short story even, unrelated to predecessor and successor, and wholly removed from last or next year. From the time when I was awakened by the sound of the lorries being started, to a moonlit falling asleep after midnight, I achieved absolute irresponsibility. We were of no place through which we passed; we came from vacuum and passed into it. We made no friends on the way and we sought no ties. We belonged to no order of life, we were rootless, meaningless, homeless. But we had one another, in our own caravanserai, and our life moved with us from town to town. I learnt, in those weeks, something I had never known, the nomadic sense. No liner at sea, calling at ports and leaving them, no car touring a country with nights here and there, can give one that sense as strongly as this did. For though on a liner one is cut off from the world's curriculum with a certain number of human beings, they, with their baggage and tickets, are going somewhere, are willingly or unwillingly living through a short and necessary respite. Their journey is a journey, while ours was life itself. Our homes were on our backs, as it were; we pitched our tents with a sense that this would be a daily task for ever, as though we were a desert tribe.

Of the second I wrote no less exuberantly:

> ... the England which has just been lost. Only with a child's eye did we, of my generation, see the last vestiges of it disappearing as the petrol engine won its brief war with beauty. But to me, however imaginary the picture must be, it is very clear—villages isolated with their inn

and their church as the most significant buildings in them, men with high collars and Norfolk jackets, farmers in gigs, horse-drawn charabancs. It is not the England of Dickens, or even of the later Victoria, for those are already historical. But the England which I just missed, of Henry James's novels and Conan Doyle's, in which a 'fly' would meet you at the station when you were asked somewhere for the week-end, stockbrokers wore top hats to the city, and the music halls, in which still living artists performed, were gas-lit places where beer was served at the tables of the audience and the chairman accepted a drink. There were horse buses in it, and American millionaires who wore curious clothes; there were gentlemen with generous moustaches and button-holes who tossed half-sovereigns to cabbies, there was the Kaffir boom, the Boer War, the trial of Oscar Wilde, the coronation of Edward VII, while the last of its influence went down about the same time as the *Titanic*.

But although tenting with the Rosaires meant this additional journey to the past, it was the family which drew me that summer to leave London and my flat, to hire a trailer caravan and to drive north to Yorkshire, where they were showing.

Of course I idealized them, not so much as individuals but as a tribe. They were in a tradition much older than that of the circus which (as we understand it) goes no farther back than the last century, the tradition of jugglers, acrobats, animal-tamers and clowns who have travelled the roads of Europe from Roman times, or earlier. Whether or not the Count Rosaire was in fact the offspring of a family of such people, the life, the art, the character of him and his children showed their motley and archaic descent. That enchanted me far more than the Dickensian tradition of the circus itself.

So that my appreciation of them was on two levels. First I had a philosophical and romantic view of them as rebels against conformity and descendants of the *jongleurs*, the aristocrats of the road, blandly indifferent to householders who loved them for the colour and gaiety they brought with them, anachronistic, of an immemorial heritage, heroic and humorous.

As such I would one day try to put them in a book for with no interest in the matter at all they had inflamed my imagination.

But on another level all this was forgotten in a strong and healthy love for them all as glorious human beings, in my physical enjoyment of the life I shared with them, the joy of passing day after day from waking to midnight with never-flagging gusto, taking pleasure in the small incidents and chances of their existence, being among them, being one with them. On this level each of them was very much an individual and their grandiose Christian names, Aubrey, Vivienne, Zena and the rest stood not for *them*, the Rosaires collectively, but for one or another being of strong character, each of whom was becoming a friend.

But most of all as rebels. For I saw myself, in my life and sympathies, in revolt not merely against the Establishment but against organized opposition to the Establishment. In those years for a writer to join the Left Wing movement was to conform, to go with the crowd, and I wanted more than this. Trade unionism, I believed, was only another form of orthodoxy and mine were the ideals of an anarchist. In the Rosaires' way of living, which I saw as that of an armed band moving among the orderly householders, I found fulfilment for all my immature ambitions.

I do not think I have ever been happier, more 'thrilled' in a not yet meaningless word, than I was as I covered the miles to a county quite unfamiliar to me. The war in Spain and the menace of Hitler were completely forgotten and I was going, not to paradise, that dull bejewelled place, but to Lyonesse, Cockaigne, Avalon, somewhere beyond place and time. And if that is high-sounding so were my thoughts.

[2]

I found them at Whitby, itself a place with a history running to mediaeval greatness with the ruins of its abbey still crowning the east cliff overlooking the harbour. For us it was a holiday resort and the Rosaires had paused in their summer wanderings to stay here a week or two. Ivor and Derrick rode the elephants through the town every day to advertise their presence, and posters showed the circus lions which had been trained by Martin Russell Hawkes, a Sevenoaks vicar's son, who had joined the show last year, a gentle myopic Cambridge graduate intended for the church but seduced from it by his consuming love of animals.

During my first week with them there was a satisfying 'bundle' in a local dance hall which had advertised a Circus Ball and borrowed the Rosaires' band. The Rosaire brothers cleared the hall of trouble-makers and the dance went on without further incident; their businesslike co-operation in battle was good to see. It would be exaggeration to say that the Rosaires were anti-social for in many ways they were the friendliest people, but like all nomads they knew subconsciously that their life depended on the unity of their tribe in resisting the householders.

With the circus that year were three of these who had abandoned routine and respectability to go tenting, a varied trio who had only this in common. Charles Lawrence was a cashier in a London bank within a dozen years of his pension. His face already scarred by a scratch from the leopard which he insisted on treating as though it were an amiable kitten, his skin browned, his hair grown long, his stiff collars forgotten, he would stand at the entrance to the zoo, which he shared with Derrick, shouting its attractions at the top of his voice as the audience left the big tent.

"Bears, monkeys, leopards . . ." bellowed Charles Lawrence. "Adults fourpence, children tuppence. Have your money ready, please . . ."

With his leather cash-bag over his shoulder like a bus-conductor, with his pale eyes twinkling happily, he would dole out his little zoo tickets as carefully as he had once doled out five-pound notes at the counter of his bank. Any morning, at a time when only last year he must have sat upright on a city-bound bus, spruce and polished in his city clothes, one could see him with a long rake cleaning out the animals' cages, talking affectionately to his bears and kangaroo—a supremely happy man. Frank Geddes had been the hall-porter of a big Yorkshire hotel who had walked out of a lucrative profession to run a canteen for the circus men and Jimmy Parsons was a tailor's cutter from Glastonbury who had joined as a tent-master and assistant ringmaster.

The routine which I remembered in the autumnal mists of East Kent was resumed with the bright skies and healthy breezes of Yorkshire. The elephants trundling off before most of us were awake, the Count on the box-seat of the monkey-waggon with the horses trotting behind him, the lorries and the living-waggons, blue and yellow in the early sunlight. Then the long days, each in a new village, each populated with a different crowd of curious children and their cheerful parents, each drawing to a warm close as the big tent came down after the night show, and the men walked wearily away to sleep.

I cannot remember individual villages as we crossed the moors, but they were friendly places and the Rosaires were as much at home in them as they could be anywhere. I see only glimpses and passing moments. In one, for instance, on a windless grey afternoon the Count told me some of the early history of his circus. The big top was already up; the elephants were wandering round the waggons looking for an open window through which to thrust a trunk and grope round for a loaf, the horses grazed lazily, and only a few children from the village, unable to wait for the advertised starting time of the show, peered and played round the zoo. I forget the name of the village; I forget even its aspects; I remember only a church tower with a few rooks whirling slowly round it. A dozen yards away Jim Parsons, who so little time ago had been measuring gentlemen for suits, lay stretched on the ground wearing only a pair of flannel trousers, his bare toes moving in his sleep as the flies tried to settle on them. The only sound was Martin Hawkes's patient pleading with a pair of lion cubs which had been added to his troupe of three lions, and which he hoped to put into the act next season. The Count was in his shirt-sleeves, as he loved to be. He sat on the step of my trailer with his hat down to the bridge of his nose and his dark eyes peering out from under its rim.

He went back forty years or more to the Oldham gymnasium where he had been watched by his uncle, a boxer, who had once defeated Frank Craig the Coffee Cooler. He told of early appearances on the music halls, of busking on the fairgrounds, of his negro partner who could make a poker sizzle on his lips. I listened enthralled, and returned to the present to find the whole circus ground stirring for the afternoon performance.

The daily routine never varied in essentials, from our pulling out of the field at dawn to our settling down to sleep at night with the comfortable sense that the great tent had been built up, the two shows given, the audience sent home satisfied, and the tent pulled down again and packed on the lorries ready for the morning. But each day, as each place, has its characteristics. Late in the season with the tour almost completed you might hear one of the company, for whom place-names after years of travelling had lost meaning, say, "You remember that place where Jim lost his camera?" or, "Where the elephants broke the fence down?" or "Where we nearly built up on the wrong *tober*?" or "Where we lost the monkey?" Each stop was designated by an incident, as incidents there always were.

But Beverley stands out in memory for its minster, under the walls of which we showed. All day the white cathedral had stood over the white tent, with nothing to separate them but a road that was not too busy, and a patch of grass. That slim and stately building had seemed in the lucid blue afternoon little more solid than our own flimsy steeple of canvas, for either of them might have been painted on some enormous backcloth over which real clouds were somewhat incongruously flying.

I was tired that evening, and went to bed soon after the evening show. But I could not sleep, and lay listening to the familiar sounds of pulling down. Without looking out of my window I knew each aspect of the field. There would be Ivor standing in one van receiving and piling the seating into place as the men, and a few young volunteers, handed it up to him in planks. Derrick would be over at the zoo with Charles Lawrence, getting rid of their last visitors preparatory to pulling down their own tent and shutting up the animals for the night. Aubrey and Dennis would be helping the men to pull down and pack up. Vivienne and Ida were making one of their rare visits to the cinema—'just in time to see the last film', after they came out of the ring. Ted the electrician who was Zena's husband, would be standing by the lights waggon, ready to switch off his engine and plunge the field in darkness when the work was far enough forward. All this I could follow from the sounds that floated across to me, but soon came the slow *diminuendo*, interrupted by shouts of good night as the Rosaires and the men returned to their waggons to eat supper and go to bed.

The minster clock struck twelve into a night so quiet that the hammer-strokes sounded deafening. Across the field someone again laughed and a waggon door slammed—Little Freddy, I decided, leaving the Barracks to return to his tent. Only the horses grazing near my trailer were audible now. It was so still that when someone approached I could hear his footsteps sighing in the dewy grass.

"Are you awake?" I recognized the Count's voice, and when I had admitted that I could not sleep, he added, "Come and look at this."

I got out of bed, pulled on an overcoat, and joined him. He did not speak, he did not need to tell me what 'this' was. I wondered how I could have gone to bed without realizing what was round us. The minster was lit by a bright moon, her Gothic shape all white stone and black shadow above us. Round our field the waggons stood in an untidy circle, their lights showing through their curtains, orange and yellow and crimson. I could see our waggons and the silhouettes of the grazing horses; I could hear them gently tearing at the grass. But it was the stars I looked at first, the stars and a flourishing moon, white and intense over the sleeping circus field, and the ghostly cathedral.

There were no nightingales, no summer scents. A screech-owl, a night-jar, and once a car-engine up in the silent town were all we heard. We must have stood there for five minutes without speaking, and when the Count broke silence it was not to attempt a commentary on the beauty about us, which he must have felt (as I did) to be beyond epithet, but to turn from it deliberately to recall more of his early story telling, how he he worked with Sedgwick's Menagerie entertaining the audience while the lion cage was built up for 'the Great Lorenzo'.

"There must be people who remember him," the Count said. "He was a lion-tamer of the old school and wore enough gold lace and trappings on his uniform to fit out half a dozen admirals. He had all the tricks of those days—irons made red-hot in the ring which were supposed to be for him to defend himself with if he was attacked, blank cartridges fired, and the whole thing made to look swift and ferocious. That was what people wanted in a lion act in those days—plenty of noise, roaring animals, cracking of whips, shouting, walking about and a pretence of terrific savagery. The Great Lorenzo certainly gave them it all." The Count went on to tell me how he had met his wife while he was stilt-walking in Staffordshire.

In a place called Goole he told me more. I remembered Goole because I had once stopped to ask a policeman the way and he had taken advantage of the occasion to nick me for not having a mirror and in due course I had received a summons from Goole Petty Sessions. (How aptly are your Sessions called Petty, I wrote in paying the fine.) It seemed a place of slag heaps and sooty houses but the Count's story was colourful enough and the Countess added to it with an account of how she had put her first baby to sleep in one of the swing boats on a fairground while they went into the town to entertain in the pubs, she playing the piano, the Count whistling. "The tunes we played wouldn't appeal to people nowadays, I suppose. They'd never heard of rag-time then, let alone jazz or swing music. Fred used to whistle 'The Blind Boy', or we'd sing duets—'Whisper and I Shall Hear', 'Hymns of the Old Church Choir'. They were favourites in those days."

[3]

The Rosaires were somewhat defiant about their Sundays; they felt they had earned not only rest but recreation. I had never been more conscious of the grim hold which a sterile puritan tradition still had on some of the more docile of town populations than on the Sunday when we drove into Hull, which in 1938 kept to the gloomiest traditions of the English Sunday. It was early afternoon, and the streets were empty. Forbidding and careworn at the best of times the houses now looked funereal, with lace curtains like white palls hanging in their windows and such few inhabitants as passed before them in undertaker's costume. No café was open and no cinema showed. The refuse from the customary bacchanalia of Saturday night was still in the streets. As we drove along, the sound of our car engine echoed from the sooty house walls and only once at a street corner did we hear human voices, when a sad little group of Salvationists could be heard singing a dirge of rejoicing. Smells there were in plenty, as we found when we left the car; the pungent smell of cooked vegetables rising from basements, the smell of the city's week-day traffic which seemed to hang in the streets, and the smell of stale beer as we passed the polished tile front of a public house.

For the Rosaires this was like a punishment. They had learned not to expect much from a provincial English Sunday, but at least they demanded a cinema. Carrying their own gift of entertainment, they were satisfied with very little. If a café had music and half a dozen or so of them went to it they could be happy for an hour. Anything, they said, 'to do'. Anywhere, they groaned, 'to go'. But in Hull there was nothing, there was nowhere. "It's Sunday today," we were told in awed and reproachful tones by any townsman we asked. For the citizens of Hull that settled the matter.

[4]

We had a tragedy on our show about that time—Salt killed a man. Those two elephants had character and cunning enough for anything, but this was believed to be an accident.

They were unaccountable creatures. Shown by Ivor, or ridden through the town by Ivor and Derrick, who understood them, they seemed sweet and docile as a pair of affectionate old carthorses, but if you went close to them and looked at their angry little eyes, you could not feel so certain. Their performance was matchless, but there was a look of boredom and contempt on their faces which seemed to argue that they only went through it on sufferance and on the understanding that their own demands on life would be met. These were that they should remain unseparated, have plenty to eat and be allowed to follow their own devices. The contract worked out excellently. No one would have thought of taking one from the other, they spent most of the day eating, and provided they were not a nuisance they were given as much freedom as possible.

I am convinced that Salt and Saucy were as aware of their obligations as their owners. I am convinced that they accepted this life as the pleasantest possible for beings born to their proportions. I am convinced that within those massive skulls brains as keen and as quick as their fierce little eyes were working. It has been said that the thought processes of animals are by association, never by reasoning. If that is so, the elephant comes very near to being an exception. Salt and Saucy *thought*. A creature which could put its trunk in a waggon window, open a cupboard, take out a loaf of bread, eat it and move on to explore another waggon, does something more than associate ideas. A creature which could like and dislike, give and take, respond and refuse, as these did, was no automaton. Salt and Saucy were happy—but they meant to remain so. They had no intention of being 'put upon'. They had a lively sense of what was demanded of them, and they fulfilled those demands.

The death of their keeper was no less tragic because he apparently had no connections or friends—at least none appeared at the inquest or funeral. He was a man in late middle age who had drifted workless for a long time before he came to us in the hope of a job. He had only been with us a week or two when the thing happened. Such weight and such strength as those two beasts had cannot always be controlled, even by themselves. A foot set down in the wrong place, an unconscious swing of the leg, and the frail shell of a human skull can be smashed without the least harmful intention.

Derrick was the first to reach the tent, and his description left a clear-cut impression.

"He was dead then, and she knew it. She was trying to push him down into the earth so that no one would know about it. She looked as guilty as a child. She was just standing there trying to trample him into the ground out of sight."

Ivor, who showed Salt and Saucy, spoke eagerly in defence of his charges.

"We could never be without elephants," he said. "You've no idea what a difference an elephant makes to a show. When the kids see one walking through the town in the morning it always gets them excited."

Not only the kids, I thought. For me the elephant seems the only real anomaly among familiar animals. That this great beast, whose skin and size and colour, whose fantastic shape and unwieldly yet purposeful movements mark him as a survival of another age, should exist in the modern world has always seemed to me unnatural. For other people, it may be, there are other creatures more out of place in our time, giraffes or alligators, whales or ant-eaters. For other people these may seem, more than the elephant, to belong to pre-history. But I can never see the bristly grey hide of an elephant, nor watch its wavering sensitive trunk, its monstrous outline against the sky, without feeling that this belongs to a world of creatures we have never seen, whose names end in 'tyl' and 'erm', dragons, winged tigers and mammoths, and I wonder how long this anachronism will survive.

The circus seems to bring it into relief. The monstrosity is doubly monstrous when it walks through an English village in the early morning, or trundles round the ring.

Salt and Saucy had a story of their own. They used to belong to George Lockhart, and had been a part of 'Lockhart's Cruet' of four elephants—Salt, Pepper, Mustard and Sauce. The original George Lockhart, who had shown elephants for years, and had toured the world with his famous beasts Boney, Molly and Waddy, had tried to retire, it seemed, but like so many circus people had been unable to keep away from the ring. He bought his 'cruet' of four elephants from Hagenbeck's, and had them delivered to his Brighton home. (A wonderful firm, Hagenbeck's, in those days. An English circus had only to order half a dozen lions trained to do some specific trick, or a troupe of performing zebras, or polar bears or Shetland ponies, or whatever they needed, and in due course the creatures would arrive at their address with one of Hagenbeck's men.) These had been quite young however, and the Lockharts had set about training them. But Mustard died of dropsy and had to be replaced, and Pepper later succumbed to the same complaint. Advice from the London Zoo about the cause of these fatal attacks made Lockhart order the exhumation of Pepper— no small task, one would imagine—and there was a post-mortem which led to the discovery and cure of the disease.

There were many stories of the stampedes of the 'Cruet'. The troupe had been increased to six, and Lockhart, father and son, had a good many trials and embarrassments in travelling with them. They tried every means of checking their dashes, but none was wholly effective. Finally Salt led a stampede in which the elder Lockhart was killed by Saucy. So this was not the first man who had lost his life through our two creatures.

"But they're quiet and sober now," Ivor used to say, patting the hairy foreleg of one of them.

I used to wonder. I would sit on Salt's back—one could scarcely call it riding him—and feel as comfortable and secure as in an armchair on the ground. But I did not, I am amused to notice now, fail to have a photo taken of myself in that position. I probably smirked a little to think what more staid members of my profession would think of that.

[5]

I cannot imagine now why I left the Rosaires and returned to London. I could have finished the tenting season with them and heard the rest of their story. Perhaps it was conscience, a contract or debts. I know I hated going and remember miserably packing to the familiar march played for the entrance of the elephants.

Coming away from the circus was like leaving a theatre in which one has been lost in a fine play to find that life has continued in its sordid way in the street outside and that one must immediately take up its burdens.

Hitler had been ranting that summer at rallies, at diplomatic meetings, wherever he could raise his flat unresonant and fiercely rasping voice—will any of us who heard it ever forget it?—and Beneš had ordered partial mobilization.

Two young RAF men to whom I gave a lift as I came down through Lincolnshire were cheerfully confident that war was coming. But the RAF was ready for it.

"We think we've got better planes than they have," one of

them said exultantly. "You'll see when it comes. We'll shoot them out of the sky."

"Don't believe it when they tell you we're not ready for war," said the other. "The RAF is, anyway."

I gave them, in a conversational way, the pious cliché of the moment.

"Let's hope it won't come, anyway."

No less chattily they echoed this, but without the smallest confidence and not much warmth. They were in their early twenties and we all talked nonsense that year. One of them wrote to me after war had broken out—from Norway.

CHAPTER FOUR

Fleet Street and Ireland

I HAD not yet learned the lesson, hardest of all for one of my temperament, volatile and versatile both, that the writer's business is to write and forget the journalistic kickshaws, the broadcasts held to be worth while as publicity, the speeches at literary luncheons, the promotion of improvised gossip paragraphs and the appearance of his portrait in the press. I have no firm opinion even to this day of the commercial value, if any, of these things, but I am sure they are not worth the creative writer's own time and energy. A whole career can be made from them, especially since the coming of television, but it is the career of a Popular Figure not of a man trying to perfect his own form of art, and concern with such antics never improves the quality and very rarely even the sales of his books.* But in that year I was much concerned with them. I had come to London, I told myself, to further my career, and it did not occur to me that the only form of careerism for a writer was literary, however unspectacular the rewards.

I had published a novel at the beginning of the year called *Rule Britannia*, a gentle satire of English life seen by a French boy staying with a family in Beckenham on the 'exchange system'. By the simple device of making one of his young hosts a hearty clubman and pub-crawler and the other an ardent left-winger I had fired a few shots at both forms of fellowship and I find now from an old press-cutting book that predictably the critics of the left-wing papers were amused by my portrait of Dick and his friends, while those of the popular

*It is notorious among publishers that books by world-famous film stars, actors and actresses, television or radio personalities rarely have sales proportionate to the celebrity of their authors.

press found my sketch of a Bloomsbury party irresistibly funny, but nobody rooted more than faintly for caricatures of himself. The reviewer of one paper, the *Llandudno Advertiser*, cannot have had much time to spare with his review copy for he wrote: 'A fine book about British shipping may be found on the shelf this week, it is "Rule Britannia" by Rupert Crofte-Cooke. Rupert Cooke is well known for his sea books, but this book surpasses any that he has previously written.'

This book interested a playwright of the time who wanted to dramatize it and a desultory acquaintance followed. Merton Hodge was a New Zealander who had written a highly successful play called *The Wind and the Rain*; he was also a doctor, one of the many who have left the practice of medicine for the chancier rewards of writing. A dressy, painfully correct little man, he disapproved of my diverse and unaccountable acquaintanceship and lived contentedly in theatrical society, a diner-out, a recognizer of faces at the Ivy, a first-nighter, very severely a gentleman, the last person for whom one could have foreseen a future as a pitiful alcoholic. He returned from America on the outbreak of war to do hospital work and this, during the blitz, broke his resistance. He never recovered his talents and died in the 1950s forgotten as a playwright, a sad little biography.

Merton was a homosexual of a kind with which I have never had much patience, the discreet and respectable who waste too much of their lives trying to conceal their nature from observers. He lived in a charming flat near Victoria Station and I went there for several conferences over the dramatization of *Rule Britannia* which came to nothing.

But he gave me tickets for a play of his that was running at the Comedy Theatre. It was called *The Island* and I remember Godfrey Tearle playing rather erratically the part of an army officer and Grizelda Hervey looking lovely, and May Agate with all her shrewd talents, but of the play itself nothing remains.

[2]

I wrote no other book till I went abroad to do so in October, and in the meantime concerned myself with miscellaneous and rather shameful fringe activities.

A kindly publisher of the time, Geoffrey Bles, had taken me to the Dutch East Indies Club for lunch—the curry was superb —and proposed that I should write a book called *How to Get More Out of Life*. He was jealous of the titanic sales of an American production called *How to Make Friends and Influence People* and he mistook my unquenchable gusto for a knowledge and mastery of life's varied pleasures. It was a shallow little book I wrote to fulfil the contract we made and Geoffrey Bles was disappointed in it but when it came out that July it was reviewed very widely because it gave every critic a chance to air his own prejudices, tastes and interests as facetiously as I had aired mine. It will be scarcely credible to anyone concerned with such things today that no less than eighty-nine publications in Great Britain and Ireland reviewed that three-and-sixpenny clothbound pocket-sized book but that even these gave it sales of less than five thousand. My bill with Durrants Press Cutting Agency must have been considerable that year.

Then I was given the chance of writing one or two feature articles for the *Daily Mirror* and grabbed it without hesitation though it meant doing—less gushingly but also less successfully—the kind of thing that was giving Godfrey Winn the beginnings of his reputation. I did not write about my mother or my dog but almost as embarrassingly of circus freaks and being in the lion's cage. I would go down to the *Mirror* offices with a list of proposed subjects for articles which Anthony Clarkson in a few moments' discussion would reduce to one, and that a possibility merely. I met Hugh Cudlipp and William Connor (Cassandra) and David Walker and they all seemed intimidatingly hard-boiled, self-assured and competent and made me feel like a sentimental amateur, which indeed I was in their world.

I can see now why I achieved no more. I did not realize that successful feature articles, like successful romantic novels, can never be written tongue in cheek. They may be second-rate, badly phrased and banal but they must be sincere. A cynic might add that a good editor is one who recognizes sincerity however clumsy the expression of it; might also think that the toughness of journalists is a façade behind which they weep and rejoice with the people whose lives they seem to report so unfeelingly. I had secret snootiness about it all which invalidated what I wrote. Some of my articles just got by, perhaps because the young men running the *Mirror* were a kindly crowd and took the trouble to get what they wanted from me, but in reality I was a fake. Even the picture which illustrated my two-page spread about being in the lions' cage was a fake, for there was a movable wooden partition between me and the lions and this could be discerned until a friend in the photographic department of the *Daily Sketch* removed it, amused that the picture should be published in the *Mirror*.

Then at Tony Clarkson's suggestion I wrote an article called *Ought I to Adopt a Child?* This was right up the editorial street and brought in something like five hundred letters. I was a bachelor, I said, without responsibilities. Was it not my duty? etc. People wrote offering their children for this dubious opportunity, some enclosing photographs; and from very shame I began seriously to consider adopting a small boy named Barry whose parents said he was charming but that they were just not interested in children. Fortunately I went no further and it was Tony Clarkson, the apparently hard-boiled Fleet Street man, who went down and investigated the case.

At the time, the big type and pictures with which my articles were presented and the satisfaction of finding that I could write this sort of thing at the same time as I was reviewing novels for the *Tablet*, selling short stories to the *Evening*

Standard, broadcasting in the *In Town Tonight* programme, writing for a publication devoted to men's clothes and getting a large press for my silly little book of popular philosophy, must have fed my vanity if not my pocket. I saw myself as a famous young writer, though I was not so very young and have not the temperament for fame. But I was happy that year, rushing about, busy over nothing, going out at midnight to buy the next day's *Daily Express* to see what James Agate had said about my book, keeping Richard Parker busy with 'pieces' to type for a number of periodicals, planning to go abroad again.

I liked to feel unliterary and boasted that except for Louis Golding, with whom my anomalous relationship continued, I had not a friend in the writing profession. I remember a lunch given by Douglas Woodruff, the editor of the *Tablet,* at which Hilaire Belloc was more than usually expansive and spoke of Lloyd George as a 'common little man' and of course dominated the occasion. I ought to have been at ease with the Catholic intellectuals of my own age who were there, like Christopher Hollis and Robert Speaight, but I have always found wit of the academic and superior kind hard to take and could not resist unforgivably reminding Speaight that he had once opened a novel set in Argentina, which he had not visited, with the memorable words—"The angelus was sounding the hour for taking maté . . ." That did not make me popular with the brilliant young Catholics.

[3]

My old Lanchester car never recovered from pulling a heavy home-made trailer caravan to Yorkshire and back and I decided to give it in part exchange for a new Opel. This was a more momentous step than it might appear for there was an outcry against the importation of cars from Germany which was held to assist Hitler in his rearmament programme. It was said that hundreds of small Opels were lying unwanted on the docks although they were being offered on the English market at bargain price. Cases of sabotage were reported and the owners of Opels found their tyres slashed and their paintwork damaged in car parks.

That was enough for me. Anything which offered good value for money, as this did, and was generally frowned on appealed to me at once and I bought the standard model for £108.

That was a remarkable little car, slippery and swift in traffic and easy to handle on the open road. It was light as a biscuit tin having no unnecessary fittings or falals, but larger than the seven horse power cars of those days. I drove it mercilessly in half a dozen countries till war broke out then left it uncared for in an open-fronted lean-to for the duration, bringing it back to life in 1946 and driving it for five years longer about London and through Scandinavia. I suppose my purchase of it may have given the Nazis a little of the foreign currency they needed for armaments but this was before Munich and before the in-famous *Kristallnacht* of November that year and it was still possible to see Hitler as a noisy and ambitious dictator who would not lead his country into war.

It must be difficult for younger generations of motorists to realize the sense of personal mobility a small new car could give one in those days. It is only a very small exaggeration to say that in London one could speed from one point to another with scarcely a moment's hold-up and park anywhere for as long as one liked. To a Londoner of today it would seem like having wings. The Opel would stand at the kerb outside my flat and I would race off to leave it outside a Soho restaurant where I ate or at the very doors of pubs I visited. I was only once stopped by the police—for exceeding the speed limit in Hyde Park, and I used the car every day till the instalments ran into arrears and it was seized from outside my flat and secreted somewhere on Brixton Hill until I paid what was owing. With

Dingo beside me, bright yellow against the grey of the car, I would go through the silent streets of the city at night, down to East End pubs, across the river to the Waterloo Bridge Road, anywhere suggested to me by a companion. This I realize now was a joy of its own which has gone for ever, easy locomotion in a city. As I toil from one traffic block to another, unable to stop within a mile of my destination because there is no parking place, I think with affection of those days and nights in the Opel unhampered by the necessary restrictions of today.

There were incidents of course. On a night of deep snow at a corner of New Cavendish Street I drove into the flank of a new Rolls Royce belonging to a bullion broker which had emerged from a minor road and we ceremoniously exchanged cards like two intending duellists.

Another occasion is more memorable but only for a snapshot it left in my mind. I was driving up from the bottom of Knightsbridge to Hyde Park Corner when during a momentary traffic hold-up the face of a cyclist appeared at my window. It was not a pleasing face and it belonged to a tall heavy scowling young man in a tweed jacket and dark grey flannel trousers.

"Do you *usually* cut cyclists off?" he asked with the unmistakable sarcasm and authority of a policeman.

I was, in fact, particularly considerate towards cyclists who were even then being pushed off the roads. But I had never seen this one before and disliked his approach.

"Oh, invariably, if they get in my way," I told him.

"I'm a police officer," he said, threateningly.

"Yes, you look like it."

The traffic was moving on and I went with it. But I turned back to see him bent over the handlebars pedalling furiously to catch me up at the next lights. It is that picture which remains. Sweating, glowering, determined to have the last word, he used all his energy to pedal. It is thirty years ago and within two years of that summer afternoon he probably faced the blitz with heroism. But I can still see the sweat on his forehead and in his eyes the fury of an animal cheated of its prey.

But I slipped across on the amber lights and never saw him again.

[4]

Then of all unlikely and untimely suggestions came one that I should spend some weeks in Ireland. It was made by a friend of six years' standing named Ned O'Brien. During one of my leanest times—in London in 1932—he had been as the ravens to Elijah the Tishbite and brought me 'bread and flesh in the evening' for he worked in a restaurant as a waiter and used to knock off a daily packet of provender for me. Now he was a steward on a Union Castle boat but had spent the takings of his last voyage and wanted to go with another steward to home in Thomastown, Kilkenny. If I would drive them down to Fishguard, they said, they would have enough money to make the rest of the journey by boat to Rosslare and then by train. I could stay with Ned and his family.

Madness. I was almost penniless and had urgent work to do. But I had never been to Ireland and this would be experience and pleasure in one, the most attractive combination I knew in those irresponsible years. I could get a tankful of petrol on credit and perhaps raise a pound or two for expenses. Had I not determined that my life should be so planned that I could drop everything at a moment's notice to follow my curiosity elsewhere?

Hitherto Ireland had meant for me a number of quite potent but somewhat contradictory influences. As a very small boy I remembered at the house of one of my hearty sport-loving Taylor uncles the arrival of a large hamper containing ducks, a ham and several pounds of butter, rich ochre in colour. It appeared that my uncle went over to Ireland yearly for the fishing and had made a bargain, advantageous for both parties, by which he posted at intervals parcels of used clothing collected from the family in return for which a farmer's wife sent him these splendid comestibles. Ireland had still been regarded by that stockbroker uncle of mine as an inexpensive playground, with excellent shooting and trout fishing, inhabited by quaint peasants whose dialect the poorest mimic could reproduce so that funny stories of what Paddy said were repeated in Edwardian smoking rooms.

When in my teens I wanted to become a Catholic I learned something of Irish history which I used with partisan abandon in lively arguments whenever I could get someone to defend the Protestants in Ireland against me. But this did not make the country real to me or give me any true appreciation of its heroic past. Only through literature had I some inklings of real sympathy and that stopped short of James Joyce's *Ulysses* which bored me. I could quote whole passages from James Stephens and Yeats, and the playwrights Synge and O'Casey were heroes of mine. But Ireland was to me a cause rather than a country. If I tried to imagine its life and landscape it was with the sentimental idealization that was cultivated by most Englishmen of my generation—the population consisting of lovely girls with wild-rose complexions or men who never spoke unless in lines out of side-splitting comedy, wore funny hats and carried shillelaghs, the landscape one of dark lakes in the shadow of ultramarine hills dotted with picturesque small cottages known as cabins, the only traffic a procession of donkey carts on their way to market, the diet one of butter, cream, potatoes and trout washed down with potheen. The oddest thing about this curious picture, as I realized after a few days in Kilkenny, was that it was not so remarkably far from the truth.

We drove the 250 miles from London without incident, except for a stop at a Welsh pub in which voices were raised in seemingly unrehearsed part-songs. The Welsh male voice, I have always found, is more virile than the Irish and seems to come from the genitals. This group of hairy-faced Welshmen stood round the bar and shook the rafters with their deep sexy singing and we were sorry to leave. Funds would not run to our taking the car across and we left it garaged in Fishguard and after a storm-tossed night in a stuffy saloon reached Rosslare and at last Ned's home in Thomastown.

Almost immediately the most hackneyed dream of Ireland began to come true. Ned's mother was a tall work-worn Irish peasant woman who cried with joy at the sight of her son and quickly produced a vast breakfast of bacon and eggs with the wonderful home-made bread found nowhere but in Ireland in such perfection. The home in which she had brought up a family of six was one in a row of workmen's cottages but its rough stone-work was two or three centuries old. Thomastown was on the Nore, a market town with a ruined abbey. Through its streets sheep and cattle were driven noisily and one really saw donkey carts and shillelaghs. There were a number of ruins in the district, their fallen state attributed to the very hands of Cromwell. During our first walk we met by the river an old poacher with a face blotched and lined with many years of hard drinking who winked in cunning glee to Ned and promised to bring us a few trout for our breakfast in the morning—a promise that was kept before we were up so that we ate the most delicious of all freshwater fish with our morning tea. The landscape in every direction was of a green so lush and brilliant that one thought—even if one managed to avoid using the expression—that this really was the emerald isle.

[5]

This was my first visit to Ireland and except for a few drives with a farmer friend of Ned's I remained in that one obscure town. To this day I have not seen the Georgian beauties of Dublin or the lakes of Killarney or any of the tourist attractions.

Yet I think I learned more of Ireland in those weeks than I would have learned by touring. I could not have chanced on a place more truly Irish than this market town in the centre of a wide agricultural area, small enough for everyone to know everyone else with nothing in it to attract tourists or sightseers, but a great deal to attract me.

With my two friends I would go for long walks down the river, finding a few hundred yards from the town that we were alone in an almost uninhabited area. Calm evenings of long watery sunsets, in which the ruined tower outside the town rose dark and menacing by the waterside and Ned would tell us, with a mixture of humour and awe, of the ghost story attached to some uninhabited cottage we passed. (Any premises that were vacant, I concluded, attracted a ghost story.) Then this reminded Ned of one nearer home.

"Have you heard the cobbler?" he asked me because I was sleeping in the attic. "You haven't? But everyone who has slept in that room has heard him. Well, the English are deaf to such things. Its only the Irish who have the ear for them."

"Who is the cobbler?"

"He's been dead for a hundred years or more but you can still hear him if you listen, tap, tap, tap all night, for ever trying to repair his shoes. He lived in the house next to ours and hanged himself in the attic beside yours and every night since he has come to work at his last, poor soul."

Ned had not seemed a superstitious man in London, but here there were buildings he would not pass after nightfall.

Those walks along the river remain clearly in my mind, but no less clear is the great shell of Mount Juliet, a fine eighteenth-century mansion some miles from the town which had been burnt down 'in the time of the throubles' and stood among its beautiful gardens, a stark and blackened pile with no roof. The gardens had been kept under full cultivation ever since the disaster, perhaps in readiness for the rebuilding of the house. It was a hot August day when we went there on hired cycles and doves cooed persistently about us and there was no one to interfere with our sun-bathing on the lawn where garden parties had once been held for the English colonizers. In every direction the green hills rolled away from us unbroken by any sign of the industrial age.

In the town there was a feast-day and a religious procession chanting its way across the bridge, a strangely foreign scene against those house-fronts which could have been in a West of England town. In the afternoon in the fields by the river there were sports and games and a very spirited jig competition in which group after group, many of the boys wearing the kilt, climbed to a dais and performed. As Filson Young, writing of folk-dances, said: 'In Ireland there is but one dance —the jig, which is there, however, found in many varieties and expressive of many shades of emotion, from the maddest gaiety to the wildest lament.' The emotion of the young dancers that summer afternoon in 1938 was of uninhibited joy, and that was infectious.

There was no political bitterness perceptible among the people of Thomastown. There were some who did not altogether approve of Ned with his anglicized ways and manner of speech but as foreigners and guests his friend and I were exempt from criticism.

It was less than four months since the signing of the Anglo-Irish Agreement of April 25 (1938) which with only a few reservations made Ireland an independent republic and de Valera was at the height of his popularity. One heard of someone in the town being 'a great de Valera man' but there was little animus in conversations on politics. I was a great de Valera man myself at that time and until he destroyed his image in my eyes by sending condolences to the German Embassy in Dublin on Hitler's cowardly death in a funk-hole. No talk of neutrality or protocol could excuse that gaffe and after it I abandoned most of my juvenile hero-worship for de Valera who had led the Irish out of great tribulation. But then his picture stood on many cottage sideboards along with that of a son of the house in the uniform of the British Army or Navy.

We returned to England with our last shillings spent and faced a long, hungry, smokeless drive from Fishguard to London until I remembered we could take the Cheltenham–Oxford road and so pass the Puesdown Inn near which I had lived for three years. The Curtis family welcomed me and gave us lunch, drinks and cigarettes on credit and so, my friends said hyperbolically, saved our lives. I was so grateful that I gave the debt priority and settled it within a fortnight. Such improvidence and recklessness in matters of money and obligation were a part of my life at that time and although I do not think that anyone eventually remained unpaid I was pretty incautious with other people's money. But it was this neglect of my obligations which enabled me to do pleasant impulsive things like leaving for Ireland without preparation. Damn it, I should never have been to Ireland if I had not made my creditors wait a little longer than they bargained for. Even now I cannot sort out, with any confidence, the ethics of that.

CHAPTER FIVE

Munich Crisis and Provençal Song

BACK in London in early September I was soon made to realize that events in Europe could no longer, by even the most blindly optimistic of us, be shrugged away as the sensationalism of foreign correspondents or the blood-curdling stories of returning holiday-makers. These were always 'eye-witness accounts', a term immediately suspect when used in public then and thereafter. But now, though the stories had not all suddenly grown credible, there was undeniable reason for alarm. Even a man leading as selfish and absorbing a private life as mine had to recognize that Hitler was not a marionette who had them all at it in Germany, raising their arms and bellowing "*Heil*", was not an irrelevant buffoon to amuse the cartoonists, but a menace to the blissful continuation of things as they were.

Whatever pretensions I had to esoteric knowledge based on my recent travel in Europe, I was very much a typical popular press-reading citizen in this, as I found later when I met in the army the men who had been duped no more than I. The events leading to Munich alarmed me as none of the portents which had gone before had done, and wishful thinking was useless against them. When Chamberlain announced peace in our time I was as relieved as everyone else.

Perhaps no event in history has led to more boastful hind-sight than this, more claims to have seen the folly and wicked-ness of appeasement. It is all very well to talk of Guilty Men and to see in the wretched Chamberlain a credulous and cowardly old temporizer who betrayed us. We were all (or very nearly all) guilty men and should have the courage to admit it. The rapturous crowds at the airport who cheered him hysterically as he waved that ridiculous piece of paper were not exceptional people—they cheered for all but a tiny minority* of not necessarily wiser Britons.

Was this, after all, so surprising? Moving behind clouds of propaganda, Hitler could not yet be seen with any certainty as worse than a rabid patriot determined to redress the wrongs of Versailles. All he wanted, he reiterated, was the union of all German-speaking people within the boundaries of the Reich, and with them the members of no other race. Could it not be held natural that the Sudeten Germans, divided from their fellows after the First World War by an imposed boundary, should wish to return? It was to be Hitler's last territorial claim. Oh yes, we know it all now, what had already happened to the Jews in Germany and what was to follow, what happened to us and all the world when Hitler was given his way. But it is contemptible and vulgar for us, who actually or metaphorically cheered Chamberlain as a peacemaker, to claim foresight and superhuman perception at the time.

I remember those days very clearly. For the first time since reaching the years if not the attributes of maturity I felt that I had lost control of my own life. Reading the newspaper, listening to news bulletins I searched for any detail in them which gave hope of peace. For that had become the issue in my mind, not peace in our time, not peace with honour but simply No War, so that we could all continue with our occupations and pleasures. Trenches in the park, visits from air-raid wardens to fit gas-masks were not quite real for if war came it would end everything. Trenches and gas-masks would be equally useless in Armageddon. There were, for most people I believe, the simplest of alternatives—peace at any cost, at any sacrifice of face, at any nation's expense, or war, when life

---

*Though in that tiny minority, I have since been interested to note, were almost all the autobiographers of the future, almost every politician who lived to remember the occasion and a great number of writers who all claim to have seen in the black-clad person of Chamberlain not a peacemaker but the angel of death and destruction.

would be at an end. By the time war came we could see less extreme possibilities. We were prepared—far too late of course —to defend what we called our principles, meaning ourselves and our freedom, from the boredom, squalor and humiliation of Nazi rule. But at the time of Munich we saw only the issue— to be or not to be.

So the days passed in strained anxiety. For the last time I saw politicians as masters of the fate of peoples, not miserably bewildered men at the mercy of theory, precedent and chance. I may have smiled a little at the appearance of Chamberlain, that scrawny neck and ugly mouth and the expression of a startled cab-horse but I did not question his sincerity. Somehow I hoped he would save us to continue whatever we were doing when this irritating German had started screaming about the Sudetenland.

A letter came from my German friend Ernst Thoma. He, like many of his countrymen, probably the majority, hoped as ardently and as helplessly for peace as I did. Our letters read as though we were both living under the same threats. "I still believe Hitler to be a man of peace," wrote Ernst. "He thinks he can get what he wants without war."

The truth was that it took more imagination of the darker kind than any of us possessed to conceive of the psychopathic horrors in the diseased mind of the man who had been allowed to achieve autocracy in Germany. We did not want to believe that war would come, we could not believe that it was already inevitable because a cowardly rabble-rouser supposed he was born to usurp the powers of God.

On September 23, the day on which Chamberlain flew to Godesberg on the second of his journeys of appeal, I was book-ed by the BBC to jockey a programme of Czechoslovakian folk-songs, some of which I had heard in Prague that January. This had meant a pleasant consultation with Paul Selver whom I had not seen since he edited the *New Coterie* ten years earlier, and with his help I had a good selection of records. It seemed likely that the programme would be cancelled, but during the morning I received a call from the BBC. It could proceed, they said, but there was one folk-song the title of which must not be given in English. It was called *Sad Times are Now Beginning*.

I remember sitting in my flat listening to Chamberlain's announcement on the 29th, in his voice a ring of pride and pleasure at bringing good news. I was alone with Dingo and the house was silent. "Herr Hitler . . ."—the voice of the one-time Lord Mayor of Birmingham sounded respectful, but confident. There was to be peace in our time. All I had for noble sentiment, for shrewd percipience of disaster or for exaltation was a quiet uncomprehending "So *that's* all right . . ." and after a moment, " . . . thank God."

But within a few days I was carried away by the general reaction. Finding ourselves still alive, unbombed, in no immediate danger of war, we could join those Members of Parliament of all parties who had cheered so rapturously when Chamberlain was invited for the second time to Munich but found now that after all he had not been so clever. Churchill denounced the Munich Agreement and Labour and Liberal members discovered that Chamberlain had 'betrayed and abandoned' Czechoslovakia. Everybody became immensely wise and resentful. Whatever we were during our Greatest Hour two years later we were not very a heroic nation at the time of Munich.

[2]

I decided to go abroad at once. I planned to stay in Erstein, a small town in Alsace, where my French friend Robert Cahiza was working, and without the distractions of London write a long novel, but I had never seen Provence and undeterred by the prospect of several hundreds of miles motoring in the Opel I set out for St Remy.

Speeding down the long straight roads of France I forgot

the strain and anxiety of the last weeks. Born with a love of autumn above all other seasons I drove under the reddening trees and gloried in the sense of freedom which the possession of a car and a few pounds gave me to go wherever I wanted and stay as long as I liked.

On my second day I stopped to give a lift to two young hitch-hikers and found they were students from Paris making their way to Marseilles. One was named Paul Sée and he was the son of a certain Léon Sée who had been manager to Primo Carnera. The other had completed, or was on leave from, his military service in Algeria. Beyond a formal 'Do you think there will be a war?' a primary question, almost a greeting, between strangers at that time, we did not discuss politics. They both talked well, as young Frenchmen so often do, and the distance was easily covered.

I had chosen St Remy almost at random because I had heard that another young novelist, John Lodwick, had worked in it all the summer. However, I postponed my stay there and drove Paul Sée and his friend to Marseilles and spent some days and nights exploring the Vieux Port.

[3]

It was perhaps fitting that I should come on the Vieux Port a few days after the Munich crisis when Hitler's armies of hypnotized young men were already mobilized, because within five years that ancient rat-run would be obliterated on German orders.

It was not the first *quartier des bas fonds* I had explored for I knew Hamburg's S. Pauli, the Boca of Buenos Aires, the Rue de Lappe district in Paris and the Barrio Chino of Barcelona, but it was the most dedicated to vice and crime. Even in the morning it had a squalid and bedraggled air like a whore waking in a soiled bed.

The streets were so narrow that climbing from the dockside a man could touch the walls on both sides of him while down the gutter in the centre of the paved alley filthy waste and urine would run between his legs. The architecture was not of the windowless Moorish kind found in many old quarters of southern Europe but of the early nineteenth century, tall shuttered houses rising to sharp roofs. This part of the town could have changed little since Dumas' time—in the daytime deserted and rather sinister with eyes peering through the shutters and lean dogs sniffing round garbage, but in the evening waking to a rabid gaiety and the competition of pimps looking for victims. There were a few brightly illuminated entrances but those more popular with furtive pleasure-seekers were the shadowy ones in which could be seen only an old *madame* beckoning from behind the blinds.

I went with the two students to see a blue cinema and wondered why the unbelievably silly films shown in these places always seem to have been made in the early days of cinematography and with grotesquely ugly sets. When afterwards we became *voyeurs* of the real thing, watching through hidden peepholes, we grew hilarious and were afraid our laughter would disturb the hero in the next room. (The woman knew we were there and waved gaily to us from behind her client's front.) It would not have taken much to disturb him— he came sliding into the room and forgot to take off his bowler hat which remained grotesquely on his head throughout, though a pair of grey woollen combinations was revealed which, with his walrus moustache, made the whole thing like a pornographic episode in a Mack Sennett comedy.

It will be thought that I am lying, or at least inventing retrospectively when I say that I had a premonition about the Vieux Port—no vision of the flames that would destroy it but a feeling that I should never have another chance to see it. When eighteen years later I wanted to set a novel there, bringing my story to a climax in the last hours before the Germans blew it up after giving its twenty thousand people a few hours' notice, I could not have done so but for those days in October 1938.

I spent time in Marseilles itself and think now that like most great European cities rebuilt since the war, it has lost a character altogether less impassive than the glass and concrete mass, orderly and expressionless, which I find in its place today. The Rue Cannebière, famous in the last century for its length and width and illumination, was then still a great street, but nowadays it is one of several hundreds in the world with dimensions just as impressive. I went to a department store there and was horrified when a few days after my visit the whole building (and others adjoining it) was destroyed by fire during its busiest shopping hours, seventy-five people being killed. Though air-raid casualty figures were soon to make this loss look trivial it was gruesome at the time, as death by fire or water must always be, whatever means of mass destruction we discover and use. I had left the city before I heard of the fire but it took on nightmare qualities in my mind. Even today, though I know it well now, Marseilles has for me a lurid and melodramatic attraction, with suppressed hysteria under its dull glaze. Other Mediterranean cities—Barcelona, Naples, Beirut—have this air, but in my mind at least Marseilles for all its commercial magnitude, is touched with blood and fire.

[4]

St Remy, on the other hand, was a tranquil village built round an open *place*, with a busy communal life of its own. Today, if I could find such a place as St Remy was then, with the best hotel costing less than a pound a night, excellent meals included, I should settle there contentedly to work for a month, make friends in the cafés at night and take walks in the autumnal countryside about it, but then I was restless and full of curiosity, about Provençal customs, dance and song—of which I learned little—and about Avignon, Arles and Les Baux, which I visited.

From Avignon I kept for years, until I revisited the city after the war, only a nightmarish recollection of being one of a pack of tourists being driven through the empty halls of the Palace of the Popes by a relentless guide who stopped in each great featureless chamber to explain its function and history, then translated his words into English. There was not a piece of furniture or a picture in the place and the walls were broken only by high windows. Through one chamber after another we were herded and there was no escape for even if I could have broken away from the rest I could not have found the way out. Perhaps I had lunched too well, perhaps I resented being conducted at all, but for years afterwards, even after learning in the army what waiting about, transfixed with boredom, could mean, I had no doubt that the dullest hours of my life were spent in that sightless tour.

At Arles I saw the Roman remains but the amphitheatre, which I compared inevitably with that of Merida, seemed altogether without the ghostly life I remembered in the Spanish ruins, perhaps because it is occasionally used as a bull-ring. Here again sightseeing was organized and exploited while the great touristical invasion of Spain was still a dozen years ahead.

But Les Baux—I could appreciate that. I had not yet seen any of the human eyries which crown steep hills in Mediterranean countries, and Les Baux seemed one of those unlikely places which for want of adjectives we call beautiful or unique but which have something supernatural, something that belongs neither to men who built the fortified village on a rocky peak, nor to God who raised the peak to overlook hundreds of square miles of land and sea.

In that long-lived autumn—for it was far into October now and the sun was still dull gold over the burnt Provençal plains —Les Baux was almost unvisited. In the ruined village only a score of human beings remained at night, while in the surrounding country there were no habitations but farms. (In the grounds of one of these was an elegant Renaissance Pavilion from which the owners of that time, to their amazement, derived the benefit of an occasional tip from people who wanted to see their old barn and would pay something to be allowed to do so, though grandfather had always used it for storing corn.) Now at the foot of the hill is one of the twelve restaurants in all France which are given three stars in the *Michelin Guide* (Baumanière) and advertises as specialities *rouget en papillote, gigot d'agneau en croûte, poularde a l'estragon*, together with a *vin du pays*, not dignified by that name before the war. Even up in the village there is La Riboto de Taven with only one star and three sets of crossed forks. When I drove up the winding hill to the village I was the only motorist to have done so since noon and among the ruined buildings at the peak I found no one but two young Germans labouring under the rucksacks they had toted up the hill.

As I came towards the broken walls of Les Baux I saw over to my left caves hollowed out of the cliff by men. These had once lain under the castle walls as dungeons or cellars and at their entrance was a large notice-board the words on which delighted me—*Les Maisons des Troglodytes*, Troglodytes' Houses. I do not know whether the name was inspired by academic humour or was a piece of semanticism from some solemn archaeologist, but it came back to me with sinister associations during the blitz, two years later.

From the topmost crest of Les Baux I saw (indicated by one of those useful beings who feel a compulsion to share their knowledge with you) the Crau, the Camargue and as far as Aigues Mortes. There was a sheer drop from here and a marauding Viscount of Les Baux, Raymond de Turenne, was said to have watched with glee his unprofitable prisoners thrown from it. I am always sceptical about that kind of legend for with that drop, if there had not been a story of a sadist tumbling people over, one would have been invented. I did not want legend, anyway. I was content to sit on the stone battlements and look over all Provence, as it seemed, stretched out in the afternoon sunlight.

[5]

Remembering those days—or weeks, was it?—at St Remy and my exploration of the surrounding country, I can understand how men from the north of Europe have dreamed themselves into various conceptions of Provence, some seeing it as a romantic land of troubadours, others as a country of hot passions and violent death. The fierce colours in Van Gogh's paintings, the pungent regional dishes, the heady wines, the powerful scent of wild herbs on the hillsides, the lusty bronzed people with their intense stares, everything seems more trenchant and robust than elsewhere in France. But for me that autumn it was a calm and homely land of long sunsets and crisp autumn mornings in which I forgot entirely the near-hysteria of London a week or two earlier. I left it meaning to return in the following year, yet with half a premonition, I think, that I should not come again.

CHAPTER SIX

Alsace and Switzerland

WHEN during the war we each had our private war aims, I felt secretly but strongly that what I wanted most was to do as I could in the last years of peace—set out in a car to go wherever on the map of Europe inclination or the promise of experience might take me, staying a night or a month in any inn I chanced on, making acquaintances, finding good food and wine in unexpected places, or following the recommendations of *Michelin*, unintimidated by time or responsibility, as free as a human being is able to be. It would be ten years before this became possible again and then only partially so for we were checked by currency regulations, the Iron Curtain, post-war police officiousness, the price of petrol and the enormous cost of living. Nor did even this modified liberty last more than a decade or so for now the motor-car by its sheer multiplicity has ceased to be a comfortable means of transport in Europe and currency restrictions are back with increased malignance.

But in that autumn, between the Munich crisis and the war, France was still a playground and other countries, though some felt threatened and two had fallen to Nazism, continued to move to the sound of revelry. My drive up the eastern boundaries of France to Alsace, and afterwards into Germany and Switzerland, was roses all—or nearly all—the way.

It was in those years that I began to be familiar with aspects of gastronomy which can only be learned from the productions of professional chefs. Brought up by my father—gourmet and gourmand too—to appreciate the best in food and wine as we know them in England, myself a cook since boyhood with some flair for recognizing quality both in raw

75

materials and in the arts of preparation, I had with time and travel come to gain a useful understanding of food in restaurants, a specialized knowledge related to but not identical with gastronomy. The language of the food snob and the wine snob I found to be a distortion, or an exaggeration, of the terminology used by professionals in the catering and wine trade and I had little use for the more flamboyant examples of it to be heard in England, the excessive and unnecessary use of French terms, not those appearing in the menu where they are appropriate but those bandied about in conversation where they are pretentious. Most of all I had learned that the true gourmet was often inarticulate and that the man who really cared for wine usually said little more of what he was drinking than that it was good or poor, too old or too young.

But I was still at the age (when will I grow out of it, I wonder?) of experiment, and drove with the *Michelin Guide* on the seat beside me, stopping for lunch at recommended restaurants and ordering the speciality of the house and the *vin du pays* when there was one, eating the local cheeses, or dawdling through a long *table d'hôte*. In Marseilles I had eaten *bouillabaisse* three times in three different restaurants—the dish differed with each but was always delectable. *Bouillabaisse* was not a snob food then, faked and imitated and even tinned, but a Marseillais or at most a Provençal dish, usually for special occasions. I have eaten makeshift versions of it since, and camped-up elaborately served fish stews which go under its name in expensive restaurants but for one reason or another I have never enjoyed it so much.

Now I was on the road and making for the Dauphine and Savoy, where the food was of the kind found in mountainous districts, game, trout and delicious local cheeses, all things I *love*. (I use a word forbidden to us as children if spoken in relation to food though not if applied, more hypocritally, to aunts and uncles.) Driving up those far from perfect roads and stopping to eat with an appetite made lively by the mountain air, swallowing wine in manly quantities without fuss or discussion, spending no more than a pound a day however vastly I enjoyed myself, I was, if I had only known it, taking advantage of the last days of France as she had been since Edward VII as Prince of Wales showed the English there was paradise across the Channel.

This was still an epoch in which wise purchasers went to the places that produced certain articles to buy them at their best, when those staying in Devon or Cornwall posted to their friends a jar of cream, while from Yarmouth might arrive a box of bloaters or from Strasbourg a fine *foie gras*. In Grenoble I bought what I was told by guide-books to buy, gloves and chocolates, and both were superlatively good.

While still in my teens I had spent a summer month in Aix-les-Bains, that gay little Alpine watering-place between the Mont Revard and the Lac de Bourget, Lamartine's lake. It had not yet been vulgarized by the visits of Stanley Baldwin, and in 1922 I thought it the most romantic place in the world and with a French boy of my own age swam naked in the aquamarine lake, climbed the Mont Revard, cycled among the vineyards, dismounting and praying at wayside shrines, lived in what seemed to me a grand hotel, and ordered a button-hole of *fleurs d'Aix* (a bright pink erica which grew among the rocks) to be sent me daily from the market. This was because I had read that Oscar Wilde placed a standing order with a florist for a daily *boutonnière* for himself and one for his coachman. I had no coachman and I wore my own even in the lapel of a blazer, but it all seemed very fitting and necessary to a boy who had just published his first book of poems. Now I decided to return to Aix-les-Bains and drove there from Grenoble.

I found it a bright and pleasant little town, picturesquely situated, as they say, between mountain and lake; but we cannot go back to boyhood and its glamour was gone. The Beausite was no more, and there were no buxom girls in Savoyard dress selling *fleur d'Aix* in the little *place*, while the elderly American visitors I remembered, more like the Southern gentlefolk of Dickens's time than any way-of-life American one sees today, were all dead or spending their last earthly holidays in Florida.

Then at Belfort on the way north I had a car smash. The unpleasant things that befall motorists on the road are never their own fault, as I know from the thousand wearisome stories I have heard of them, and I believe that I am the only writer to have admitted in public that his own irresponsibility and fool-hardiness brought damage to another.* But I am not going to admit the smallest blame for what happened in Belfort. Oh, no. Even today I can see the long anserine face of a man who bashed in the side of my elegant little Opel and feel a hot flush of anger.

I was in the approaches to the town on my own side of a clear road, doing less than thirty miles an hour when a few yards ahead of me a car parked on the other side without warning semi-circled into my path in order to follow my direction. Impact was inevitable and though neither of us suffered any physical damage both cars were badly damaged, my light-bodied Opel more than his lumbering and elderly Citroen.

There was one of those discussions. The man was a doctor and made some play of being on his rounds. He evaded the two rhetorical questions—had he looked at the road before turning out and had he given any signal—and mumbled only the ancient defensive accusation that I was going too fast. This simply was not true. Even the spectators told him that and pointed out his own folly, becoming so abusive of their townsman that I left them to take over the argument while I gave details to the police. Then with chagrin and fury I drove on, ashamed of my battered car, till I reached Colmar and lunched at the Maison des Têtes, one of the few restaurants of those days which survives under its original name, and ate *choucroute* and drank a bottle of Alsatian *Riesling*. So when at last I came to Erstein where my friend Robert Cahiza awaited me it was with no pride in the first new (as opposed to secondhand) car I had ever owned.

The Purple Streak, 1966.

[2]

Robert Cahiza was one of an international trio who were my friends when we were in our twenties and remain my friends today. There was John Hitchcock the Englishman, Ernst Thoma the German, and Robert Cahiza the Frenchman. How typical each was of his country I could not realize at the time, but today it seems they might have been created by a novelist to stand with their wives for the best of the conventional type of each race. They have never met one another for I have known each of them in his own country, but they have certain attributes in common. All their marriages are enviably successful and happy, all their children now in their twenties, following their parents on what my father would have called 'the right lines', John having a son and two daughters, Ernst a daughter and a son and Robert two sons. What is more remarkable is that each of my friends, in spite of any influence from my own feckless-ness, has reached eminence and the company of Croesus, all being presidents, directors, chairmen, what-have-you, of vast commercial concerns out of my ken. If I had been looking for winners, as a young man, I could not have picked better. I was not. I was not even consciously looking for friends, though in that I was immeasurably lucky for each of them was, and is, an interesting man in his own right, not merely for me because of old associations.

In 1938 I had known Robert Cahiza for eight years. He was still in his twenties but had a character integrated and balanced beyond his years, which I took to be natural in a Frenchman, for I still believed that French youth was by cir-cumstance more sophisticated than our own. 'They develop sooner on the Continent' was an article of faith to the Victor-ians and Edwardians.

Robert was working as an accountant for a wool-spinning concern in or near the little Alsatian town of Erstein, twenty-three kilometres south of Strasbourg. It was a cheerful place of cobbled streets and sharp gables, attractive in the Alsatian manner, very much of its province. We stayed in a comfortable pub in which I had a room warmed by a tiled stove, for I meant to work all day and there was snow on the hills around us. Alsatian wine, I was delighted to find, was bottled in the long-necked flasks familiar to me in Germany, and local wine, at least of the quality which I could usually afford, was indistinguishable from hock.

We ate in the kitchen-dining-room in which there were three or four tables for guests and I still remember the *choucroute*, the astonishing variety of *charcuterie* and the ungenteel but welcome quantities of food offered to us.

Everyone in the town seemed to be blond, more so than in the German Rhineland, and all the males wore cropped hair so that when I went to a barber who understood only Alsatian I came away shorn like a caricature of Fritz. The Ersteiners were friendly and welcoming people, but few of the townsmen whom I met in the pub at night spoke French or German, preferring their own speech which was neither, so that I was saved from 'having on opinion' on Alsatian affairs, the small number of pro-Nazi autonomists and so on. For me it was a slightly unreal country with bright little fairy-tale villages and storks' nests on the chimneys.

At week-ends I drove with Robert to mountain villages or to one of the famous restaurants on the French side of the Rhine to which the Germans crowded to escape the stoical conditions of the homeland. In these there were formidable *table d'hôte* menus, more common in good restaurants then than now, and on one occasion at least we ate our way through seven courses.

[3]

The novel I planned to write at Erstein was to be *long* above all things, though I daresay I chose more flattering adjectives in my own mind. Walter Hutchinson still controlled my chances of advancement in terms of sales and royalties and he or one of his deputies had insisted that it was time for me to finish with *jeux d'esprits* and write a big, serious, 'important' book, offering to spend more money on advertisement if I would make it over 120,000 words in length. It appeared that there was a fashion just then for *big* books and Hutchinson from his Hampshire home had decreed by telephone to the offices of his subsidiary companies that all authors under contract to him were to be encouraged to produce these. Quite apart from the fact that there must be a *natural* length for the interpretation of any honest novelist's theme or idea, I was and have remained incapable of achieving a long novel and like others of my generation have been, by Victorian standards, little more than a short-story writer.

But I had not the self-critical acumen to perceive this and was still at that stage in a writer's life when he believes everything is possible to him. I set about writing *Same Way Home* with enthusiasm and confidence. Its central idea was to be an enlargement of the plot of a play which had been produced on a Sunday night at the St Martin's Theatre some years earlier, but there was much scope for expansion. It all seemed easy and tempting, a matter of sufficient ink and paper.

I do not know how much other authors remember of the actual writing of their books—perhaps it is clear to them in each case; there they sat, looking on that prospect, using that pen or typewriter, looking up those reference books, working so many hours. Only in the case of two of my novels have I the least of such recollections, but *Same Way Home* was one of them. Waking to the crisp Alsatian morning, going down to breakfast to give the landlady time to do my room, then warmed by the great stove, sitting at a bare oak table and scribbling on the lined paper I always used with a giant Waterman fountain-pen. The only book in English I had with me in Erstein was Dostoievski's *The Brothers Karamazov* and I read a little of this before each stint of work to give it impetus—a fact unguessable from the character of the book I wrote. Robert would come in after his office hours and we would go down to the main room of the inn where there was an even larger stove and we would order a bottle of wine before the hearty evening meal. I rarely wrote less than two thousand words a day and sometimes considerably more.

[4]

One week-end I decided to go back to Zug. Six years ago I had taught—or, as I more grandiloquently maintained, lectured—at a strange educational institute for the sons of millionaires and such high on the Zugerberg which overlooked the German Swiss town. I had passed a glorious winter there learning to ski and *luge* down the mountain, and a summer nearly as idyllic swimming in a bathing pool among the mountain pines. The experience had ended in tears and a threat of litigation, for after leaving the Institut Montana I wrote a novel called *Cosmopolis* about an Institut on a Swiss mountain and Max Husmann, the proprietor, not unnaturally, maintained it depicted his. Hutchinson had withdrawn the book and demanded the implementation of a clause in my contract which made me liable for losses through libel actions, and as a result I was still tied to his firm. But the temptation to go back to Zug was too strong and I set out for Switzerland with Robert Cahiza one Saturday morning.

This in itself seemed strange. It is circumstances which make distance, not mileage. When I had gone to and fro from London to the Zugerberg there had been no regular air service except the somewhat adventurous crossing from London to Paris and characters like Amy Johnson were still achieving 'flights' to far places. Taking a car abroad was also complicated and expensive and I had gone as a matter of course by train, first the Channel crossing, then a long overnight journey ending in local trains in Switzerland, then a tram-ride to the station of the mountain railway and finally a long climb in the funicular. The Zugerberg had seemed a remote and isolated peak in a country never before visited. It was surprising to realize that from Erstein it was an afternoon's drive.

Arrived at the Conditorei Kaiser in the town at the foot of the mountain I was delighted to be recognized by Frau Kaiser and decided to telephone Husmann whom I had last seen in Jarrold's office in Paternoster Row where we had argued furiously over the withdrawal of my book. I had always rather liked him, an intelligent Jew from the Balkans, of tremendous energy and enterprise, rather handsome in a Slav way, with no sense of humour but a gift of persuasion and some charm. To my surprise he now welcomed me and invited me to the Institut to lunch.

Snow had not yet fallen and the lower slopes of the Zugerberg were covered with orchards and pretty little dolls' house chalets. I had never approached the buildings of the Institut by car and they looked white and rather impressive in the late sunshine. They had once housed a luxury hotel which had failed and Husmann had bought the place as it stood so that the pupils, some of whom were in their twenties, occupied single bedrooms.

I wanted to know what were the effects of the Munich crisis on this. As I remembered it the boys were drawn from most European countries but chiefly from Germany and Italy. There were Czechs, Yugoslavs, a few British, Belgians (but no Frenchmen), Spaniards and Scandinavians, also some South Americans. The fees had been very high and the Institut attracted the sons of industrialists like the German Klöchner, or the Italian Usuelli, the proprietor of the Borsalino factories, politicians like Count Grandi, and a gamut of titled plutocrats. What would have happened to it now with Hitler screaming from beyond the northern frontier of Switzerland and Mussolini from the southern? The Czechs would already have gone and the Spaniards. I imagined that Husmann must be facing a crisis.

Not at all. Numbers were higher than they had ever been and drawn from as many countries. Switzerland might be guarding her frontiers and watching her declining hotel trade with anxiety but this millionaires' institute was full. It was a little less of a playground, perhaps, but that was because Husmann was in residence more. The unfortunate Swiss masters were not quite the butts they had been for the jibes of sophisticated youngsters and poker games in the *wirtschaft* broke up before midnight. But sitting at the high table in the dining-hall, eating the excellent food which I remembered, I looked down the lines of pupils—guests, perhaps I should say —and seeing the carefree faces, the expensive clothes, I guessed that assignations with the young women of Zug were no less healthily exploited while love affairs in the school itself, unregardful of racial distinctions, made for the amity of nations, at least among the young.

Husmann treated me as a respected guest, almost with the deference shown to a prospective parent, and nothing was said about *Cosmopolis* or my year as an assistant here. I realized that what I had dramatized as a turning-point in my life, my association with a mixture of races and my loss through the suppression of a book, had been no more to him than the brief employment of a tiresome assistant master and a short visit to London to discuss a possible libel. But I enjoyed my day on the mountain. Once again my passion for returning to people and places had paid off.

CHAPTER SEVEN

Germany and Paris

I DETERMINED to enter Germany. I felt very little apprehension about this but it would be like no previous visit. When I looked across the Rhine at night there were strings of lights where no villages stood, and I was told that the Germans were feverishly building fortifications along the riverside. Threats and harangues from leaders were heard in a hysterical crescendo whenever we switched on the radio and adventurers returning from Germany told hair-raising stories of arrests and concentration camps. It was nearly a year since I had travelled across the country and in the meantime there had been the immediate threat of war and the Munich conference. Had I foreseen Hitler's occupation of Czechoslovakia, the turning point and the end of hope, I should not have ventured across the frontier. But I believed that peace in our time might yet prevail.

I had known the Germans for twelve years as amiable and gentle hosts and I could not believe that they had suddenly become sinister bullies, suspicious of every foreigner, who would resent my driving in an Opel car to visit my friends at Kassel. Yet I felt it would be like entering a fortress and I too was on my guard.

There was a ferry—still running, I heard with some surprise —between Erstein and Ottenheim, or as I thought between one line of fortifications and another. Mine was the only car to be embarked and caused comment. At a Customs point on the other side I was held up for some time while an immense woman in uniform went through my papers and gave me additional forms to fill in and questioned me severely about the reason for my visit. But once on the *autobahn* I had a glorious sense of speed and freedom. It was the first time I had been able to travel with my foot hard down for lengthy periods without pause.

I passed nothing or almost nothing but a string of army lorries, though I travelled for many miles at speed on the grim deserted road. Or that is as I recollect it. When I left the *autobahn* for a village to get some food and drink I saw on the doors of the first inn I found in large uncompromising letters *Keine Juden*. Turning away in disgust I went to another bar with a similar placard *Juden nicht gewunscht* and realized that it was no use looking for a pub without these obscene signs. I went in but told the proprietor how I resented having to do so, on which he replied sadly, "We can't help it." "We have to obey orders," much as every cornered Nazi has said in self-defence ever since.

On to Kassel where all the men and most of the women seemed to be in uniform of some kind. The pleasant town in which I had stayed with Ernst Thoma before and since his wedding was an armed camp. '*Heil Hitler*' was shouted not with good humour or with defiance but with solemnity from which all the friendliness of a greeting had gone. The citizens of Kassel were in earnest now.

"Can you still get butter?" I asked Ernst's wife Clemens.

"Some," she said and would not enlarge on that.

[2]

There was no restraint between Ernst and me for all his Brownshirt uniform hanging in the cupboard. I knew that for him, working in the great locomotive factory of Henschel, it was as obligatory as trades union membership in England today, I also knew that he had been reprimanded for lack of enthusiasm several times. What I did not know, and what Ernst did not tell me until thirty years later, was that he had been particularly reprimanded with some danger to himself for being 'ill' on the night of November 9-10, a week or two before my coming. This was the night of the most unholy pogrom before the war and only because he had secured a certificate from a sympathetic doctor did he escape serious consequences. "Why didn't you tell me?" I asked him when we were talking over old unhappy far-off things in 1967. "I think perhaps . . . I didn't want to talk of that night," said Ernst and we discussed it no more.

I suppose some news of it must have reached me in France but like so many people who knew the Germans before this blackguardry was whipped up, I simply could not believe it and put it down to counter-propaganda. I saw no sign of it during that visit.

No, Ernst's Brownshirt jacket did not make me feel uncomfortable because I had known him before there were brown or black shirts or any sign of the swastika. But the town and particularly the block of flats in which Ernst lived disturbed me. Radios were played loudly to demonstrate to anyone listening that they carried only German programmes. My movements were watched each time I went in or out of the flat, not by police spies but by suspicious or merely inquisitive neighbours. Collectors for the Winter Help Fund (that rotten swindle) had a buy-or-else manner and there were so many pictures of Hitler that the features seemed to writhe at one from the hoardings. I was never questioned or molested but Kassel became odious to me.

"Can't we go away somewhere for the week-end?" I suggested to Ernst.

"Where can we go?" he asked, and though the question looks desperate and unhappy on paper now, it had no undertones of such meaning then.

I suggested we should drive to a village called Kreuzberg because I remembered it with affection from my journey to the East on *The Man in Europe Street* trip. Ernst agreed and we left on Saturday afternoon.

I have recounted an incident of that evening elsewhere, but the whole episode was revealing. Kreuzberg was farther away than I judged and it was past one o'clock at night when we drove up to the pub in which I had passed festive hours with my circus friends a year ago. We found the car park full of coaches and lorries and the *gesellschaftzimmer* crowded with Blackshirts and Brownshirts in uniform. They were making for Weimar where Hitler was to speak on the next day and they were converging from different parts of the country for this act of devotion. Within ten hours they would be in that vast sea of faces which surrounded the rostrum, yelling, bellowing '*Heil*', raising their arms in energetic salutes, cheering at intervals throughout the wild diatribe which their hysterical little leader was even now preparing. They had to travel all night because for security reasons no one would be allowed to enter the city after daybreak. Meanwhile they were drinking rum and hot water and were somewhat flushed by the alcohol and the stove-heated room after their cold drive through the darkness.

But they welcomed me, an Englishman, breaking in on their cults and they boasted with gusty good humour of their devotion to their tutelary god. It was bad luck, they implied, on any race who had not got a Hitler to worship and had to be content with prime ministers and such—for they could not believe that any nation could manage without hero-worship. There was a tricky moment when one of them bought me a drink and raised his glass to Hitler. Mindful of Ernst I could make no gesture but said—"I drink to peace." "It's the same thing!" said the Blackshirt beaming with rum and generosity, and I was glad to let it go at that.

A few rounds later they grew more insistent. Didn't I think it was a fine thing, their Movement? In an atmosphere so amicable, myself warmed with rum, I said perhaps more than might have been wise in other circumstances.

"What I can't understand," I told them, "is that you all have to guard your speech so much. I can"— I was becoming rhetorical—"I can sit by the fireside of an English inn and say

I think the Prime Minister should be shot and the Throne be replaced by a republic and no one will interfere with me."

There was a rather dramatic silence. Then a little man who had spent some time in England and had remained silent throughout the argument said with a grin—"Yes, but you could not be sitting by the fireside of an English inn *at all* after ten or eleven o'clock, could you?"

I was shattered. But fortunately perhaps the laughter was on me. From the land of closing hours and petty regulations where police waited at the doors of licensed premises not to hear subversive talk but to summons a landlord for serving a glass of beer three minutes past the scheduled time for closing, where hot rum in the small hours would be a deadly sin, where there was freedom of speech but restricted freedom of action, I was dumb. I can see their faces now, rubicund, blue-eyed, proud and happy; they loved me for laying myself open for their retort and wanted, they said, an Anglo-German alliance, wanted me to to come and hear Hitler, wanted me to understand what he meant to them. It was an educative hour.

Later I went with Ernst to the attic where we were to sleep and found it under bare rafters with a pinewood floor and those vast red eiderdowns like rising balloons which were laid over the beds in rural Germany at that time. I wanted to ask him about the crowd downstairs, what they did besides cheering for Hitler, what proportion of them he would say were fanatics and so on, but he made a sign to silence me. Attic walls were not thick and here as in Kassel there was always someone listening.

Only in the car next day were we safe from eavesdropping. I asked, with particular point because I was speaking to a German of military age as well as to a trusted friend, that question which we all put several times a day in 1938.

"Do you think there will be war?"

Until now, and in recent letters, Ernst had always said no. Now he was more hesitant. Looking back on that morning I suppose that while in one sense it was a very ordinary young man with no particular foresight who answered, in another it was some millions of German people with all their secret anxieties and forebodings.

"I don't think so," he said slowly. "I can't imagine it. But I am frightened by the fact that it all depends on one man."

"You mean that?"

"Of that I am sure. Of nothing else. Imagine that—the peace of the world depending on one individual. If he keeps his word to us there will be no war. If he is mad or bad there will. I still don't think he is. He can't be! Some of his prejudices are irrational, some of his schemes are out of date. But I can't believe he will do this. To us, let alone to the rest of the world."

"And if he does?"

"If he does they will follow him. *We* will follow him because there will be no choice. You saw those fellows last night? They're hypnotized. If he tells them today to start marching against France, Russia, any country, they will cheer him as much as ever . . . and start. There would be no hope of any kind of opposition. There *is* no kind of opposition. I should go with everyone else. And Hans and Bruno.* There would be no choice. But I still hope he may keep his word."

That was the refrain—*his word*. Once again Ernst reminded me, though not so firmly as before, that in the German view Hitler had not yet broken it. The hopes of millions of Germans lay in that rather nebulous piece of self-persuasion. With wishful thinking as agile as our own they passed over what looked to others like breaches of faith. They clung to the fact that until now in all his appropriations there had been a German majority in areas added to the Reich. (It would still be three months before the Germans entered Prague.)

My friend was not a pacifist or any other 'ist, or a Nazi or or even an anti-Nazi, he was a young man newly married whose wife was expecting a child, whose parents wanted retirement

---

*Ernst's younger brothers. They were both killed on the Russian Front.

and peace, whose brothers were making careers, who was as lost as we all were in the maze of issues and events.

As he sat in my little car returning to his home before I should leave for mine he and I were equally bewildered, and we knew it. We know it, I think, today, thirty years later; the difference is that now we have no longer any of that pitiful human faith, described by Wells, in wise adults above the power of governments who have the problems of the world in hand.

I drove again down that long *autobahn* as far as I could follow it, then across country by greatly inferior roads to the Rhine crossing.

[3]

Alsace seemed very calm after Germany and Erstein was almost free from uniform. I worked at my novel till well into December, then left for Paris where I should stay for a few days.

I had been through Paris a score of times since that long-ago summer when I had lived in Passy and made my first explorations at night, but never for more than a few hours in passing, never with freedom to stay out till daybreak, as any healthy and fully sexed young Englishman expects to do. I did it all, from Place Pigalle to the Turkish Baths (*massage sous l'eau* they mysteriously advertised), and to St Germain des Prés which was not the tourist trap it has lately become. I had dinner at Lapèrouse, choosing of course the *gratin de langoustine Georgette*.

But it is one statement made to me by a man of my own age which I remember most clearly of all I saw and heard in those days. He was the elder brother of Paul Sée, who had been my passenger to Marseilles a month or two before. He was a very sophisticated fellow with a *garçonnière* full of attractive girls and he wore one of these tight black jackets fashionable with such young people at that time—very soigné and eloquent.

"War?" he said. "It will never come here. Not to Paris. There may be an air-raid or two—nothing more. The Maginot Line is unbreachable. Inviolable. You may be quite sure of that."

He stretched himself on a chaise-longue and twisted his little moustache as though he would be taking his ease in his smart apartment for years to come.

"It's not for nothing we've built this thing in depth," he said. "They can throw themselves against it as long as they like— they will never get through."

It sounded so assured and so impressive after the doubts of Germans. I found time to remember M. Sée in the summer of 1940.

CHAPTER EIGHT

London and Compton Mackenzie

BACK in London I found myself involved in political argument. In fact I suppose I came as near as I have ever been to that barren region of echoes called 'public life'. It was not a very close approach and I drew back sharply when I saw where I was being led, but I faintly heard its reverberations.

The book I had written about my trip through ten European countries in search of the man in the street was published on the very day of Chamberlain's return from Munich with Hitler's signature to a peace pact, and what had been little more than a stunt, a piece of journalistic ingenuity, was seized on as serious evidence that things were not as bad as they seemed, that people wanted peace, that perhaps even the dictators wanted peace, and so on. The very prominent press criticism the book received makes wistful reading now and I am amused to see that Malcolm Muggeridge in the *Daily Telegraph* gave it the best part of a column and said that 'it was a useful and readable addition to the ever-growing literature of foreign affairs', and that R. H. S. Crossman in the *World Review* told his readers that it was worth reading for the information it gave. "He does manage to give an excellent impression of the average fair-minded Englishman abroad, listening to chance acquaintances in the café or the restaurant. His pictures of Sudetenland, Hungary and Fascist Italy are excellently done, and he rightly stresses the contrast between public opinion in Italy and Germany, and the far greater freedom of expression permitted in the former country. A lightweight book but good of its kind."*

*This was offset briskly by the Left-wing press—"Dear Croft-Cooke, you are much more amusing, and infinitely more intelligent, when you write about darts", said the *Tribune*, while the *Daily Worker* told me that—"Such deductions say a lot for the warmth of the author's heart but singularly little of his head."

It began to seem that my book threatened to make me, in a small way, that loquacious monster 'an expert on foreign affairs'. My ideas were in pitiful confusion. I wanted to share Ernst Thoma's not very strong faith in the peaceful intentions of Hitler. I was guilty of a great deal of wishful thinking and I had little political knowledge. Yet I was consulted quite seriously. I was supposed to know something. I was 'an optimist'. Intelligent men tried to find reassurance in my opinions. I do not think I was aware that I had no opinion worth a light. I was the blind leading the blind without even a sense of direction.

I was asked to speak at a Foyle's Literary Lunch on 'The Press and Germany', a dangerous subject at the time. The day's theme was the Freedom of the Press and Christina Foyle had gathered four speakers and a chairman, two of them Members of Parliament, one of them a famous editor, another a controversial columnist and myself. Beverley Baxter was in the chair, and Wickham Steed, Dingle Foot and Hannen Swaffer were to precede me, a piebald and motley selection. What was I doing in that galley, anyway, I wondered as I drove the Opel, still showing scars, to Grosvenor House.

It was chaos from the start. Wickham Steed who was formerly editor of *The Times* for three years and edited *The Review of Reviews* had been a warm man on foreign affairs in his youth but had become a bearded Jeremiah monotonously —though with reason—crying Doom. He was tartly pulled up by Beverley Baxter for wandering from the point of the debate. He lost his temper, his head, his audience and his place in his notes, and sat down in confusion. Dingle Foot was conscientious and wordy and we turned for comic relief to Hannen Swaffer, a malicious old stick who used to walk about Fleet Street in old-time actor's drag, wearing a stock and a broad-brimmed black-hat. He wrote crapulent gossip for a Sunday newspaper "I disagree with everything you say . . ." he shouted in a flat voice and kept us waiting for the inevitable rhetorical sequel ". . . but I'll die for your right to say it!"

"And now," said Beverley Baxter with bright Canadian patronage, "a gentleman who will talk about the freedom of the press in Germany," and beamed contemptuously.

It is never much fun explaining what you *don't* mean, what you do not propose to say and what you have no intention of being mistaken for. But I managed this and steering between Nazi sympathies and what I saw as anti-Teutonic sensationalism in the British press, got by pretty well. It is a pity I had not seen the inside of Dachau which was in full swing at that time or realized some of the horrors of *Kristallnacht* which had come only a week or two before. I could scarcely have talked of sensationalism then—the British press was if anything too benign. But wishful thinking can enslave the mind. I wanted desperately hard that there should be no war and almost convinced myself, as I knew that many unfortunate Germans were convincing themselves, that Hitler was a man of peace. I did not, thank God, say so in so many words but my implication was that the press—for this was a debate on the press—was determined to see the worst of Germany.

The disturbing thing, in retrospect, was that this callow optimism of mine was received by that comfortable audience with applause. I might have been a major prophet. I had said what they wanted to hear and they were grateful. But only the audience. Beverley Baxter ostentatiously congratulated me and fifty or sixty people bought my book.

Not, needless to say, Kingsley Martin. *The New Statesman* duly pronounced: "At one point a reference to Madrid and the International Brigade made me clap. A military-looking gentleman at a table near turned round and glared at me with such ferocity that I tried to hide behind Lady Rhondda. Peeping out, I found that he was looking up my name on the list. The speech that this gentleman and many others most approved was by Mr Rupert Croft-Cooke, who denounced the press for atrocity-mongering about Germany before the last war and again today and suggested that the Nazis had never had a fair deal in this country. How odd it is to hear all this analysis of the

dangers of press misrepresentation, which no one would listen
to while democratic Germany asked for justice, now dished up
in the interests of aggressive Fascism!"

I saw my danger. I should be forced to defend a position
which I did not hold and from simply thinking that war was
not inevitable, that Hitler and the Germans might still want
peace, be mistaken for a full-time Nazi apologist. Already
Admiral Sir Barry Domville, a fine old simpleton who had
been Director of Naval Intelligence Division and was now head
of an Anglo-German friendship association, had asked me to
lunch and shown me a friendly telegram from Goering. (When
war broke out he declared that the King's enemies were his
enemies—but they arrested him under 18b just the same and he
was sent to the Isle of Man with Mosley.) Most mysteriously
I had been approached by a representative of Goebbels named
Rosen who asked me if I would like to write some articles.
'How easy is a bush supposed a bear' I thought, and determined that there should be no more misunderstanding. I wrote
to the *New Statesman* and Kingsley Martin published my
letter.

Sir,

Your account in 'A London Diary' of the Foyle
Luncheon last Wednesday, does me more than one injustice.
That you should describe my speech as the one most
applauded by 'a military-looking gentleman at a table
near' might be passed as polemics of a ravelled and prejudiced kind. But I really must protest at your implication
that I spoke "in the interests of aggressive Fascism", that
I "denounced the press for atrocity-mongering *before* the
last war", or that I "suggested that the Nazis had never
had a fair deal in this country". I did none of these things,
and I challenge you to produce one sentence from my
speech in justification of your account of it.

Do you share, then, the modern passion for categoriz-
ation? Because I resent certain misrepresentations by the
popular press, *must* I be a Nazi apologist? Before I spoke
on Wednesday I had already been foreseen by the chairman

and one speaker (without more reason than that I was to speak on the press in relation to Germany) as a sort of miniature Goebbels, an impression which I did a sincere best to destroy, in justice both to myself and to the Nazi regime. May I ask then, what conceivable grounds you have for stating that I dished up arguments "in the interests of aggressive Fascism"?

RUPERT CROFT-COOKE

To this was added a note which seems very moderate now.

(*Critic writes*: "I am sorry if I have done Mr Croft-Cooke any injustice. I entirely agreed with him when he said that there was an element of truth in the remark made by men in the trenches in the last war that the press had some responsibility for making the war; I have said the same thing myself many times. I was concerned to point out that it was playing the Nazi game, however, to suggest that the press had exaggerated the Nazi Terror recently. The important thing to my mind is to keep always the distinction between a mass of Germans who are neither better nor worse than ourselves and the terrible behaviour of the Nazi leaders and Storm Troopers. About that I feel one cannot keep silence though I am aware of the dangers." —*Ed., N.S. & N.*)

There was a certain temptation to me, not to support the Nazi cause of which I already knew at least that it was cruel, humourless and deluded, but to play the *enfant terrible* in derision of the Left, who dominated what there was of literature at that time and was humourless, smug and full of sagacity. The Left Book Club mentality, the poets who knew with such certainty that honour could only be found on the Government side in Spain, the political commentators to whom Stalin's purges were right while Hitler's were wrong, the pacifists who wanted to arm everyone but themselves, the academic socialists who had never seen a queue at the Labour Exchange or felt a moment's hunger, all the intellectuals whose superior knowledge was impregnable till the German–Soviet Pact was announced—I instinctively distrusted them and for two pins would have invented and voiced fascist sympathies.

But fortunately I *had* two pins, and very firm pins they were, my sense of humour and my affection for Jews who since boyhood had been my associates—my father having made many of his friends on the Stock Exchange. Guided by feeling rather than logic, by instinct and prejudice rather than thought, I was not in serious danger of seeing Hitler himself as more than a mountebank with hatred against one particular race. And in any case he would soon invade the rest of Czechoslovakia and enslave a foreign people, and beyond that there could be no equivocation.

I wanted to get away from speculation of that kind and from people prone to it, to the safer prejudices of anti-intellectualism. "Lauk a mercy on me, this is none of I!" It was time to be back with the circus.

[2]

The Rosaires' farm was twenty-five miles away at Billericay and when their tour was finished and they had taken up their winter stations with their waggon chimneys smoking happily round the house, they regarded my flat as their London headquarters. There was usually one or another of the boys, or of their friends, staying there, and my comparatively studious rooms began to resemble the living-waggon we called the Barracks during the afternoon show when everyone was running in and out to change. This in itself was delightful, but it meant also that I was drawn into circus life of a wholly new kind. Circus people travelling in isolated tribes scarcely meet during the summer, but during the winter months they become more gregarious.

I soon realized that I must abandon all hope of working for a month or two, and let things take their pleasant course. Some of the family were going up to Edinburgh to work during the Christmas season, but Aubrey was clowning at the Agricultural Hall, Islington, and Jim Parsons was working on the dodgem cars there. Friends from tidier walks of life who came to see me soon ceased to be surprised at the sight of what they called 'trapeze artists' and my housekeeper learned not to raise her eyebrows when she came in the morning to find beds, settee and chairs occupied. I myself no longer felt any alarm at the door-bell ringing in the small hours for a weary acrobat who had come from a dance, and when a most metropolitan young woman telephoned one day to ask who were those extraordinary people she had met at my flat the night before it took me a moment or two to realize what she meant. With Jim Parsons coming in every night after midnight, tired from eight to ten hours' jumping from car to car collecting fares; with Aubrey arriving with Jim in search of sleep because he had sometimes to make room in his waggon for one of his sisters who needed a night's lodging in London; with clothes and suit-cases, make-up boxes and photographs littering the bedrooms and telephone messages covering a good-sized pad each day, I began to feel myself living as much in the circus as I had been when I travelled with the Rosaires in the summer.

When the London shows opened my acquaintanceship grew, spreading out from the Rosaire family into wider reaches of the circus. At Islington there were French, German, Australian performers, as well as the Irish Baker Boys, who rode with Mills all the summer and were working at the Agricultural Hall for its winter season. Every day I met someone, introduced as always with a summarized biography and learned a little more of that life for which the word circus is used as an adjective.

There were in those days perhaps twenty or thirty circus families, the Sangers, Ginnetts, Chipperfields, Fossetts, Holloways, Yeldings, Bakers, Pinders, Cooks, Paulos, Bostocks, Wombwells, Proctors, Scotts, Alexanders, Austins, Kayes, Duffys, Chapmans, Newmans, Omeys, and perhaps a few more which escape me. They married and intermarried, and occasionally new families, like the Mills and the Rosaires, were added to them. In those weeks in London, sitting in a certain branch café of the Express Dairy Company, which had been adopted as their rendezvous (probably because it stood on the site of an earlier coffee-house they once used), or leaning over a little bar at the back of the Agricultural Hall or walking about Olympia, or gossiping late into the night at a small restaurant opposite to Olympia, at all of which circus folk collected, I heard something of their histories. How the Sangers themselves were slowly leaving the family business though the show went on; how one of the Ginnetts, Claude, had become an amusement manager and another, Frank, was an equestrian director; how Dick Chipperfield's act of wrestling with a bear had been at the Palladium that year; how Tommy Kayes was rapidly getting to the top of the bill and was at the Holborn Empire that week; how the eldest of the four Baker Boys, who had been one of the finest riders of the century, had died, and how his brothers Billy, Dickie and Pat made one of the most popular acts with Mills's; how Claude and Tony Yelding rode with them while their brother Frank was with Chapmans; how there were two Pinder's Circuses tenting, Tom's and Edward's, and two of Fossetts, Bob's and Tom's, the latter proudly horse-drawn still, and how young Bob Fossett was one of the best riders performing; how Mrs Paulo with four daughters and a son had pluckily fought all sorts of difficulties and kept her fine little show touring; how one of the really Grand Old Men of the circus was E. H. Bostock who lived in Glasgow, and one of the Grand Old Ladies was Mrs Proctor; how the Chapmans had come to the circus from showing animals, and how there had been three generations of Duffys in the business. All this I heard with an embellishment of vivid anecdote and humour, and a pride in the achievements of other performers which was generous and sincere.

Circus people, I found, were almost unaware of the 'cult' which surrounded them. The novelists and artists, the journalists and parsons, the photographers and professional society people, who buzzed round Islington and Olympia were assessed as human beings, and accepted or not according to the circus estimate of value, with an easy disregard of any other appraisement.

On the opening night of the Islington Circus all who were left of us who had been with the Rosaires went up to the Agricultural Hall. We passed through the rowdy fun fair, stopping to talk with Jim Parsons who leapt off a dodgem car and leant over the palisade, returning to collect another dozen sixpences, and came back to us as though he had never known an occupation away from the fair-ground. We saw that show and there was the opening of Bertram Mills's to see a few days later, the most perfectly staged circus in the world and that year the most exciting, with the Christianis thundering round and Charlie Rivells, the brilliant little Catalan, doing his immortally funny clowning, and young de Rivhero on the wire. I spent whole afternoons and evenings at Olympia, talking at the ring-doors to Frank Foster before he stalked out with his familiarly optative, 'My Lords, Ladies and Gentlemen . . .' or chatting with Clifford Hall who was sketching there for some of his fine circus paintings, or gossiping with Charlie Rivells. Then I would cross the road to a small café-restaurant where the Baker Boys and Alby Austin, who was one of Mills's best clowns, used to meet for supper every night. It was usually one o'clock before I set off to drive home. Whether I liked it or not, whether or not I had once disapproved of it as 'intellectual', and 'artistic', I had 'gone circus'. Even when, with some misgivings, I met Lady Elinor Smith, most articulate of circus fans, who had graduated to an interest in circus from her passion for gypsies, I did not find her in the least like a popular novelist but a friendly zestful woman who gave me a thrill of pleasure whenever I saw her.

[3]

When in my teens I realized that English literature did not stop with the 'great' poets of Palgrave's *Golden Treasury*, Tennyson, Browning, Matthew Arnold, or with the 'great' novelists in their heavily gilt collected editions, Dickens, Thackeray, George Eliot, I still did not understand that its progress (or retrogression) had been continuous. For me there were Classics and—infinitely more exciting—there were Moderns. The moderns were divided into Those Who Will Live—and the Rest, who were in the dog house. The list of poets who would Live was a very long one from Kipling and Housman to Brooke, Ralph Hodgson and Walter de la Mare. Occasionally a name new to me might qualify but T. S. Eliot never made it. The list of novelists who were both Modern and Immortal was sternly limited, consisting of Thomas Hardy, Maurice Hewlett, Joseph Conrad and Compton Mackenzie in the first four places with Somerset Maugham, E. M. Forster, Gilbert Cannan, H. G. Wells, Arnold Bennett, D. H. Lawrence, Norman Douglas, John Galsworthy, C. E. Montague and May Sinclair as (sometimes doubtful) runners-up. Henry James was American, Aldous Huxley was still an uncertain quantity, the rest were Out.

Writers were gods to me as a boy, the Classics on Olympus breathing the incense of mankind's adoration (for it never occurred to me that there could be people to whom literature was not the only way to immortality, who might think painters, composers or even soldiers or politicians were of significance in the history of the world), the Moderns scarcely less exalted, living in remote houses, the shrines of future pilgrimages, in which they were defended against vulgar intrusion, or surrounded by a romantic court circle abroad or adventuring forth to the scenes of their novels, mysterious and incognito.

Among the Moderns there was one with whom—in imagination, of course—I allowed myself a certain more intimate approach, as to a favourite saint, that was Compton Mackenzie. I knew he had been at my father's old school St Paul's and heard of the very masters who had taught him. I knew he was at Magdalen College, Oxford, after Wilde and Bosie. I knew that he had published an early book of poems, lived in Cornwall and Capri, been an Intelligence Officer in the 1914-18 war, and bought one of the Channel Islands. I had read every novel he had written.

But it was *Sinister Street* which had seemed to me, in my twenties, the most momentous event in modern literature. I find it impossible to convey to men of younger generations what this book meant to me. The tender flexible prose, full of exquisite conceits yet tough and stringent when need be, the harrowing nostalgia which even now (I read the book every five years or so) stirs emotions I cannot dismiss as adolescent, that quality of a vivid period which transcends all period, only in this, and in *Lord Jim* of the books I loved in boyhood, can I relive my early devotion to letters.

At thirty-five, in the year of which I am writing, I was a little more worldly-wise, but *Sinister Street* was still a magnificent book and Compton Mackenzie was still a heroic figure, not merely as a writer but as a man. He had not sat at his desk or quietly travelled 'for copy' like Somerset Maugham, or been a sycophant of the establishment like Hugh Walpole, or retired even from novel-writing like E. M. Forster, but was to be heard of with a jaunty beard making his homes on islands or gently ridiculing his earnest fellow writers Brett Young and Lawrence, or standing in the dock of the Old Bailey to answer a malicious charge, appearing in the kilt as a Scottish Nationalist derided as a would-be reincarnation of Bonny Prince Charlie, defending Edward VIII against Baldwin and the Archbishop of Canterbury, being rebellious, independent, prejudiced maybe, but unconquered by the times.

He had been book critic of the *Daily Mail* for some years and had given me that kind of encouragement which a young novelist so greatly needs, reviewing each of my books as it

appeared and referring to previous ones in a way which showed
that he was interested in my progress.

Now I was to meet him, and set off for the Vale in Hampstead in which he had taken a house. This would be the last
time I would 'go to meet' a writer as a disciple, as I had met
Kipling, Bosie Douglas, Jack Squire, Galsworthy and
Chesterton. Even Belloc, whom I met that year, was a fellow-
guest at a luncheon party, a very different thing in my mind.
Already I was too old for this attitude and for no one else
would I have assumed it. But Compton Mackenzie stood alone.

Now I would be able to ask all the questions about *Sinister
Street* and *Vestal Fire* that had so long puzzled me, 'what song
the Syrens sang, or what name Achilles assumed when he hid
himself among women', which café in Leicester Square was the
Café d'Orange, who was Arthur Wilmot in life, Robert Ross or
Reggie Turner, and what was the real identity of Marsac-
Lagerstrom? Was it true that Mackenzie worked only in the
small hours to the music of gramophone records and had he
left the Isle of Barra?

The questions were never asked—some remain open to this
day in spite of *My Life and Times*—but instead two facts emerged,
that Monty Mackenzie was a great conversationalist in the
tradition of the eighteenth century, and that he accepted me as
a friend.

I have known him since, in circumstances which varied from
that little Hampstead house to his home on the Island of Barra
in which I spent my embarkation leave, from the grandeur of
his post-war house at Denchworth to my own at Ticehurst,
from the Savile Club to the Quarter Sessions at Lewes, and I
have heard him talk till daylight more than once, but nowhere
has that paradoxical personality been more vividly expressed
than in the low-ceilinged room in the Vale. He was clean-shaven
at that time and looked less than his fifty-five years; the face,
familiar from photographs, had humour, resolution and the
tireless curiosity of the creative artist in its expression. He
wore tweeds of a colour called, I think, burnt sienna, and he

moved about the room actively and talked much, but asked questions, too. A week or two later he was prostrated with that form of sciatica which has tortured him at intervals since youth, and incapacitates him for certain periods in every year, though it could never be guessed from his vigorous and restless life. "Everybody," he once said, "has something which tries to spoil his life. I have been fortunate—but this is mine." He never referred to it again.

That first evening in the Vale was touched with splendour as though all that he had created, the people and the prose, were in the shadows of the room as we talked. In a sense this meeting was the fulfilment of an ambition which had been mine since a friend at Tonbridge said I ought to read *Sinister Street* because (he knew about my High Church excursions) it was about a boy like me. It was not in the least, but that was enough at fourteen and I gobbled up *Sinister Street* for the first time. But that evening was the beginning of something too, which would one day lead to a court-room in Lewes where Monty Mackenzie lightly indulged in one of the most supremely generous actions in a life of generosity. As shall be related.

We talked till nearly midnight and I remember that Philip Jordan, who was then features editor of the *News Chronicle*, came in and, hearing of my interest in the circus, at once commissioned an article on it. I drove home triumphantly.

CHAPTER NINE

Major Road Ahead

THE doubt and wishful thinking, the futile hope which I and my German friends had held that Hitler and his Nazis might not intend to make war, the silly speculations about his character, his intentions, his security of leadership, were all resolved in March 1939 when the Nazis annexed the truncated state of Czechoslovakia. Again retrospective wisdom was vociferous—everyone, apparently, had always known that Hitler would seize Bohemia and Moravia with the Skoda arms factories. Wasn't it obvious? How could anyone have been *relieved* at Munich?

For me, at least, there was no more uncertainty. Thenceforward I believed that Hitler would fight a mad-dog war with anyone who got in his way, though I had very little premonition about the total nature of that war. I still kept some elements of hope that it would exhaust itself in eastern Europe or that Nazi power would in some mysterious way dissolve, or that by some unpredictable means we should be able to hold on to our precious immunity.

But about Hitler and Nazism there was no more uncertainty or vacillation. The rape of Czechoslovakia was to me proof absolute that Hitler regarded his pledged word to the West and to the German people with complete cynicism, or as the Spaniards say more expressively *no tiene palabra*, he *has* no word. I see now that it was no revelation—the way of aggression had been clearly mapped from the first and Munich was nothing but an irritating roadblock. But at the time it seemed that this was the first positive exposure of Nazi aims.

I at once determined to put this certainty into action or at least into print. On the night on which Hitler's seizure of Memel was announced, March 15, I had a long conversation with my friend Michael Harrison at which it was decided that I should make an anthology of essays from writers of military age answering the questions Would I fight? Why would I fight? When would I fight? It would be a retort to that long-ago Oxford Union resolution "In no circumstances would I fight for King and Country". It would be called *Major Road Ahead*, a phrase quoted from a speech by Lord Halifax in the House of Lords—"Attempts have been made in certain quarters to under-estimate or qualify the Prime Minister's assurance of solidarity with France, and I am bound to say that any such attempts as those I most greatly regret, since it would be a profound error to suppose that any mental reservation of any kind accom-panied the Prime Minister's words. That declaration was indeed quite clear and quite unmistakable. If I may translate it into terms of a homely parable, it was in the nature of one of those signs which we now see in many places in the country, at danger-points on our highway system, carrying the device 'Halt: Major road ahead'."

I do not know whether the idea was mine or Michael's, probably a collaboration for it was our habit to talk till the small hours on tea brewed in the basement of his house on the other side of the Edgware Road while his wife was upstairs asleep, and we played tinder and flint to one another's ideas. He had recently edited a collection of short stories by writers under the age of thirty at the time of collecting, though pub-lishing delays caused a good many of us to be beyond that arbi-trary age-limit when the book appeared. There are several names in it which are still extant and I suppose it must indicate a whole generation of story-writers, though Graham Greene and Evelyn Waugh are noticeably absent.

That book, *Under Thirty*, is worth a moment's retrospective glance, even though I am in the midst of discussing another anthology of more concern to myself. There were thirty con-tributors and some rich youthful egotism was displayed in the autobiographical notes, several of them almost as long as the short stories that followed. Walter Allen told how he 'filled the University magazine with imitations of Joyce, Edgell Rickword, Eliot and Auden', John Betjeman how he disliked 'aeroplanes, main roads, insurance companies' and many other things including 'Tudor and Swedish building' while Arthur Calder-Marshall announced that 'to be full, a man's life must have a threefold relationship; firstly to his wife and children, secondly, to his work whatever it may be, thirdly, to society as a whole'. David Gascoyne remarked, 'Now, at the age of twenty-one, having passed through surrealism, communism, mass-observation', while H. E. Bates stated that he was chairman of the parish council, captain of the local football team and a member of the local cricket team. John Pudney had begun work at sixteen and a half and was a feature-programme producer for the BBC. Randall Swingler modestly claimed that his life had been 'very dull' 'though it has been exciting and funny enough for me'.

But what has happened to the other twenty-three? Most of them had published a book or two at the time and nearly all, by implication, claimed literature as the primary interest of their lives. We may have been a short-lived generation or possibly our future novelists were all killed in the blitz or have taken to more profitable careers than writing. Or perhaps they follow their calling unknown to me. But it certainly seems that most of them have faded out and that those who still write do not make much of a showing compared with other generations, earlier or later. We were pretty bitchy about one another, too, and our inverted snobbery as instanced in the autobiographical notes was not to be believed. Or was I a cuckoo in the nest? The only review I saw of *Under Thirty* was by H. E. Bates, one of the contributors, who wrote in *John O'London's Weekly*: "I find myself happy in the company of such writers as Leslie Halward, Walter Allen, Douglas Boyd, W. J. Beamond, Arthur Calder-Marshall, Walter Brierley, John Hampson and others who have worked as colliers, bricklayers, commercial travellers, and other undistinguished occupations. The stories of these men have an authentic punch, colour and sincerity that certain others lack. Mr Rupert Croft-Cooke's contribution, for example, is a smart entertainment piece flipped off by a magazine writer who really has no place here."

But to return to Michael and our scheme for an anthology of defiance. The great thing was speed, for who knew but that Hitler might not move decisively before the book was out? Next morning I rang up J. Alan White who was then managing director of the company of which he is now chairman, Methuen, and within forty-eight hours a contract was prepared and signed. There was no time to secure an essay from the most eminent young man in each category, but I did not do badly and ten days later, by coaxing and pestering my contributors, I delivered the copy to the publishers and the book of 184 pages in cloth covers was published just five weeks from its first conception. I introduced it with a Prefatory Letter which I addressed to Herr Adolf Hitler, Berchtesgaden, and Ruthven Todd wrote as a Socialist, John Mair (a brilliant young writer who was killed in the war) as a Liberal, Richard Parker (of course) as a Communist, Christopher Hollis as a Catholic, Emmanuel Levy, a Manchester artist, as a Jew, my brother L. A. B., who had published a novel, as a Winstonian Tory, Richard Blake Brown as a Church of England parson and a *Times* correspondent whose name I forget and who insisted on a pen-name, as a Chamberlainian Tory. This left only Fascism and there being no member of Mosley's party who was willing to say in what circumstances he would be prepared to fight Hitler, Michael Harrison gallantly took it on and wrote a most convincing piece in which he said he would fight because Hitler had betrayed Fascism! I will not, by quotation, remind any of the other contributors of what they said.

There was a good deal of fuss about it and some quite measurable headlines, but—needless to say—I liked best what Compton Mackenzie wrote:

MAJOR ROAD AHEAD (*Methuen* 5s) might be called a sym-

posium of wormwood. This "young man's ultimatum"
which is edited by Rupert Croft-Cooke, includes a lucid
and apposite prefatory letter of his own addressed to
Adolf Hitler. The other contributors consist of nine young
writers of military age and representative of most shades
of political and religious opinion. The object of Mr Croft-
Cooke's editorship is to find an answer to three questions:
"Would I fight?" "Why would I fight?" "When would I
fight?" I shall confess at once that the result of the enquiry
is disquieting because it reveals that between youth and
the major road ahead of them exists an ill-constructed
roundabout of muddled thinking which not even Mr
Croft-Cooke's own delight in the circus justifies. He
himself is always logical. Morever, he knows on whose
burly shoulders the blame rests for the present position of
youth, and he is not afraid to say so. By the time Mr Croft-
Cooke has finished with Lord Baldwin that Worcester
pearmain looks like a soggy cricket ball with burst seams
left in the corner of a playground. Of the individual
contributions, that by Mr Christopher Hollis, writing as a
Catholic, is by far the best.

[2]

Except for an occasion in my fourth year when my nurse
took me to the door of Lindfield parish church with a penny-
worth of confetti to throw over an emerging newly married
couple, I had never, even from that distance, seen a wedding.

My youngest brother was married that spring and the occasion was a splendid period piece, as my father's wedding fifty
years earlier must have been. Here was an undistinguished
family of the professional middle class gathering in strength for
a celebration which brought out the oldest members in speci-
ally purchased finery. Many old antagonisms were forgotten
or temporarily laid aside, while former acquaintances were
renewed. Here were *bonhomie* and champagne in plenty, all the
ritual of toasts proposed and drunk, an air of festivity properly

restrained, going on to the aftermath in different homes of "*Did* you see what Auntie B was wearing?" "Did you hear what Uncle C said?"

The ceremony was at All Souls, Langham Place, and in those days at that church there was a perpetual sequence of expensive weddings so swiftly following one another that the guests of a family from Virginia Water might find themselves confused with another from Tunbridge Wells. It had not the *éclat* or photographers from the *Tatler* which St Margaret's, Westminster, had, but it was on a par with St George's, Hanover Square, and smarter than your parish church, unless this stood at the park gates of a ducal estate. It was efficiently organized with a tariff of charges for organist, choir, full choir, assistant clergy and so forth and its incumbent did a full-time professional job.

Across the road stood the Langham Hotel scarcely less dedicated to nuptial celebration, luncheons before and after the ceremonies. The Langham was not quite Claridges, as All Souls was not quite St Margaret's, but it had a certain Edwardian style about it which fitted it comfortably for families like mine.

So we all gathered in hired morning suits, an essential for weddings of this category, and wore white carnations and looked smug. My tall young brother got through his part without a hitch and his bride—everyone agreed, and without hypocrisy—looked lovely, and we stood on the steps of the church for photographs and walked across to the hotel where formidable batteries of both families gathered to watch the other ceremony, almost as important as the one in the church, of cutting the cake.

They were all there, from both sides of my family. Readers of these books of mine who, I am quite undismayed to hear from librarians, are chiefly elderly ladies and gentlemen of the middle classes, will recognize every one of them, if not in person at least by analogy.

On the paternal side there were rifts and threatened lawsuits left by my volatile father which precluded certain attendances. None of the Crofts, the only clan which had men of distinction in its ranks, attended. But my two aunts, Xenia and Eirene were there, the former the widow of an elderly and wealthy dentist to whom she had been married forty years earlier for the last two years of his life, the latter the spinster who had been kept at home according to the inhuman custom of the time to look after ageing parents. They came together, a sombre pair of Victorian churchwomen in grey. As I have recalled, they had once been forbidden by their autocratic father to attend my father's wedding in the '90s and they had waited nearly half a century for this. My Aunt Eirene, with the pent-up love which had never been given to a man, chattered sentimentally, flushed with high emotion, but my prim simpering Aunt Xenia restrained her.

My father's oldest friend, Walter Smith, a Mincing Lane merchant who stood six foot four to my father's five-seven so that they used the delightful terms 'Big Sweetie' and 'Little Sweetie' to one another, was dead, but his son, the dashing Jack Smith of my childhood, was there, a middle-aged man who talked to me about our two characterful fathers. My elder brother, an ex-RAF officer of the First World War who had followed my father on the Stock Exchange, came, and my sister had left jodhpurs and riding-stables behind to appear in pretty feminine clothes wearing—of all things—a clever hat. My younger brother Laurie, who had abandoned teaching for antiquarian bookselling, came from Brighton.

My mother's family, the Taylors, were there in force. Her four brothers, all successful hearty men, had married wives of some character. I liked everyone who had married into that family, but the family itself I found pretty insufferable. Aunt Mary, the wife of Uncle Ted, the stockbroker, was to keep her sweetness and intelligence to old age, and Aunt Molly, the handsome and perpetually elegant wife of Uncle Toby, the K.C., I admired for her charm and grace. The second brother, an RAMC colonel, had married a lady doctor, my little fluttery jokey Auntie Emma, and Uncle Horace, the Chief Electrical Engineer to the Borough of Swansea, had a somewhat remote and mysterious wife called Aunt Lillian. Three of the aunts and two of the uncles were present, Aunt Molly sophisticated, beautifully dressed and charming to everyone, Aunt Emmy chattering from group to group and threatening to ruffle my hair as she had done infuriatingly when I was at a self-consciously dressy age in boyhood, and Aunt Mary, bless her, pretending she had read my books. My mother's sister Isabel— no names were duplicated, I notice—had married her cousin Hugh Shelbourne. There was Something About a Will which had meant partial blackballing of the family by my father, but my cousin Hugh was a grand fellow, born half-paralysed but never allowing it to spoil his life, and my cousin Leslie was no less likeable. Then two sisters, Edith and Freda, I detested from the age of three because of an incident described in *The Gardens of Camelot* and was to detest again, though I daresay they were worthy creatures and respected in Walton-on-Thames from which they came for their young cousin's wedding.

Then there was my mother's youngest sister, my Aunt Florrie, or Fofo as she was called, the one on the Taylor side who stayed at home to look after her mother until it was too late for matrimony. I have described her before but I cannot resist remembering her again, for she was The Artistic One, indomitably learning new skills to the end of her life. I have described her succession of addictions to the various arts and crafts of the time. There would be a smell of methylated spirits and burnt wood when my Aunt Fofo took to poker-work, and after Christmas there would be in the drawing-room of every Taylor a table or a work-box or a desk with designs skilfully burnt into its light woodwork. There would be a smell of sealing-wax when she discovered a way of making brooches and ornamenting hat-pins by mingling into opalescent globes the colours of the waxes. Wool, leather, paper, silk were all mediums in which my Aunt Fofo worked skilfully for varying periods. Raffia-work, rug-making, bookbinding—she did them all, and did them very much better than other women who had given years to one craft instead of the few months which she devoted before her butterfly mind had found a new way of making playing-card cases out of cigar-boxes, or of ornamenting hats with devices made from twisted straw or threaded leather.

There was nothing of the Pre-Raphaelite about her appearance; she was a busy white-haired, pink-cheeked woman who designed her own hats rather audaciously but wore smart costumes and discreet jewellery. In her last years my Aunt Fofo lost her sight and in her seventies resolved to learn Braille and achieved it to perfection in a couple of years, after which, starved of arts and crafts, she died. But she came to my brother's wedding still able to see a little and refusing to embarrass anyone by dark glasses.

As usual there were funny speeches, as usual the respective mothers were a mite tearful over the champagne, as usual there was not much fratting between the two families (though they were mutually approved, I think), as usual everybody said it was a wonderful wedding and went home to hang up carefully the Moss Bros suits which they would return tomorrow.

Such occasions will not come again. There are grander weddings and noisier ones, weddings for which documentary films are made opening with shots of a bell swinging in an old church tower, weddings announced impeccably in *The Times*, but families are smaller now, aunts are too busy running their successful advertising agencies or hairdressing saloons, champagne is too expensive and nuptial couples have been living together too long to make more than a formality of what is called 'the church ceremony', as though it were an archaic piece of mumbo-jumbo. In any case, within two years All Souls, Langham Place, had been blasted by bombs and the Langham Hotel was taken over by the BBC.

[3]

Another wedding, at which I was best man, robbed me of my flat-mate, for John who had been most long-suffering with all the strange beings who came to the home we shared, was married and had no use for a flat in London now that he had a Kentish cottage as home. (Louis Golding gave him an inscribed three-and-sixpenny edition of *Magnolia Street*.) I remember that a touch of contemporary realism was given to John's last night in the flat, for while we slept with morning-coats laid out ready for the occasion we were woken by a deafening explosion—or what seemed, in those happy inexperienced days, a deafening explosion—in the Edgware Road close by. Not to worry, the IRA had blown out a shop front by a home-made bomb left in a rubbish bin at the door.

I did not like living alone in the flat and quickly agreed with my friend Myles Eadon that he should take John's room. This gave a new atmosphere to the place, for Myles filled the arm-chairs with lovely girls in pretty frocks, among whom the loveliest was Pamela, the girl he was to marry in less than a year when war broke out. Myles was in the Territorial Army and used to go for training once a week—Rifleman Eadon he was called in the flat by characters who thought the rank was a joke. It was, I suppose, to most of us during that spring.

Myles was earning a living by free-lance journalism, not as I had done with literary pretensions but more actively looking for good stories undiscovered by the press. One of those dropped with a thud—the time-honoured story of the rightful claimant to the throne of All the Russias who had been saved by a soldier and brought up in secrecy by monks. Our man was guaranteed by a character scarcely less picturesque than the Rightful Tsar himself, an amusing old con man who called himself—perhaps justly—a colonel. ('Colonel' was a popular rank just then while Low was making Colonel Blimp familiar to every Londoner.) Myles actually penetrated to the presence of the Rightful Tsar and was disappointed to find he had a pronounced cockney accent, ready-made clothes and a passion for football pools and dog-racing, which did not suggest an upbringing by devout monks, but might of course have been a reaction to it. He claimed to be afflicted, however, with hereditary haemophilia (hi-*moph*-iler, he called it), from which the Tsarevich was known to have suffered. Not suprisingly Myles failed to persuade any news editor to touch the story.

More profitable was one which roused a great deal of attention while we were waiting for war to break out. It became known as that of 'the Mayfair Boys' and for two vital days Myles had what I believe is called an exclusive on it. As the heir to a marquisate and several Old Etonians were involved it made headlines in those days when snobbery was less inverted.

Myles was not a snob but he had an inherited indifference, a congenital lack of interest in any class but his own. He bore nobody any ill will, he would have been shocked and distressed by the horrors of poverty around him if he had noticed them but he knew only his own kind and behaved as if no other existed. The people of every kind whom I cultivated, down and outs, deserters on the run, friendly criminals and riff-raff from the Edgware Road, he would study as though they were zoological specimens, help them when he could afford it, ask me naive questions about them, but have not the smallest idea what their lives were like. He was a virile somewhat detached man, soigné and carefully dressed, and he introduced me to a circle of which I knew very little—though I should not have admitted such ignorance at the time—the intelligent but philistine society of young men fairly recently down from the universities of Oxford and Cambridge, moneyed, good-natured, given to fast motor-cars and debutantes, hard-living, hard-drinking, cliquish but likeable. I frequently went with him at night to a club called the Supercharger run by just such a man as these named Robin Hanson. Was it in Montpelier Square or Mews? Somewhere off the Brompton Road, I think. "I shall go to the Bahamas if war breaks out," I remember one of the members saying between games of darts. "And remain there till it finishes." He had time to train and be killed in the Battle of Britain. Rowland Winn, a very different person from the Lord St Oswald of today, a politician lamed by the war and a serious Joint Parliamentary Secretary and Lord-in-Waiting to the Queen, voiced no such sentiments but did not boast on the other hand that he would join his father's regiment, picturesquely named the 8th King's Royal Irish Hussars in the first week of war. I liked these men, mostly a few years younger than I, more typed, less experienced but more sophisticated.

It was not among them that I made two friends already officers in the RAF, Dick Cross and Tony Lambert. They, like the two aircraftsmen to whom I had given a lift in Yorkshire, were so confident of our superior air strength that they positively wanted to 'get started' on the destruction of the Luftwaffe, and I believe it was this optimism, as well as their magnificent courage, that gained for them the Battle of Britain. They simply did not believe that German planes or pilots would have a chance against them. They were both killed in action, Dick in the Battle of Britain, Tony in North Africa.

I think it may be said, in the language of the public school common room, that Myles 'improved the tone' of my flat. I certainly had fewer chance acquaintances (I had once asked the entire Saturday night gathering in the Fitzroy Tavern back for a party) and liked Myles's mother so well that I used to cook for her when she visited him, and was devoted to Myles's fiancée and *her* mother. But I still took pride in the diversity of my friends, their classlessness, their unconformity, believing somewhat ingenuously that mine was a truer socialism than that of the Intellectual Left.

There was, for instance, an impecunious Catholic of uncategorizable origins who would crop up every few years with fabulous stories of what he had been doing in the meantime in his personal war against starvation on the one hand and conventional employment on the other. He had worked in the editorial department of one Catholic newspaper and solicited subscriptions for another, both for brief periods until his inevitable dismissal for devoting his time to discussion of Russia and the universe. He had sold vacuum cleaners and told more satirical stories of his training than Julian Maclaren-Ross; had joined the army for a time but his gift for narrative and theory in conversation had not been appreciated. He had been a schoolmaster in preparatory schools but had never lasted out a full term, had addressed envelopes, drawn the dole, washed dishes, done everything but steal or beg, for he had his integrity. When writers had done these things they gave brilliantly humorous accounts of them to the public; my friend kept his stories for me and I could listen to him for hours on end. He drifted through life, indomitably good-humoured, quite without self-pity. I remember meeting him again after the war and finding him unchanged, though he had added a job as assistant master in an English school in Buenos Aires to his triumphs. It had lasted longer than most jobs because having paid his fare to South America the authorities were unwilling to send him home immediately on discovering his wayward temperament.

Then there was an Anglo-Chinese soldier, brought up by Dr Barnado's Homes, with only a faded photograph of a Chinese seaman and a story of a mother who never revealed her identity to serve as parentage. He spent his leaves in my flat and later I was proud of having been something of a foster-father to him, for he won the Military Medal in North Africa and went on to the East to suffer, without damage to his morale or courage, three years of daily torture as a prisoner of the Japanese.

There was also Neddy, with whom I went to Ireland, who came whenever his ship was in, and an Irish mechanic from the mews below my flat, and an unsuccessful middle-aged burglar who told good stories of his life in prison, and several others who, while the Rosaires were away tenting, used my flat as a harbourage.

CHAPTER TEN

Italy

In the early summer (of 1939) I accepted an invitation from a progressive travel agency looking for publicity to accompany, with my secretary, one of their motor-coach tours of Europe. It seems an unlikely and frivolous enterprise to have undertaken in 1939. Moreover, I find it scarcely credible today that the promoters should have been so confident of the future that for the sake of nebulous benefits in publicity they were willing to sacrifice their receipts from the two front places in a coach on one of their most heavily booked tours. We should return, if we did return, on June 3, or as I know in retrospect exactly three months before the declaration of war.

By a fortunate chance a booklet issued by European Motorways in 1939, *See Europe from an Armchair*, has survived. There was a choice of sixteen tours to all parts of Europe lasting from ten to thirty-seven days, and each tour left three times during the summer. The Grand European Tour, for instance, through Berlin, Prague, Vienna, Budapest, Venice, Rome and Lucerne, was due to leave on August 6 and I cannot help wondering now if it took off.

The idea was that you took your place in a comfortable vehicle in London, were transported on a round of the best hotels in each stopping-place—and they were the best hotels, as the *A.A. Foreign Touring Guide* for 1937–8 confirms—saw every 'sight' *en route*, and were brought back without any of the irritations of travel to London.

The tour I chose was the Italian. It included, as the leaflet says: (1) The Motor Tour, (2) First-class steamer travel, (3) First-class hotel accommodation and meals, (4) All hotel gratuities, (5) Sightseeing, guide and entrance fees, (6) Services of courier, (7) Supply of Motorways' trunk, (8) Supply of special Motorways' map. The cost of this, for its twenty-five days, was forty guineas, so that I was being given eighty-four pounds-worth of free travel and accommodation and in spite of certain reserves about 'conducted tours' and travelling in a char-à-banc could scarcely refuse it.

Besides, I knew almost nothing of Italy, having been no farther south than Milan, and although I did not think that the sweets promised me in the booklets "Rapallo via Alasio (lunch)", "Pisa visiting the Leaning Tower", "Day in Florence sight-seeing", "Afternoon in Siena sightseeing", three days in Rome, "Naples sightseeing", "Naples–Perugia picnic lunch", "Morn-ing in Assisi", Ravenna–Venice via Ferrara Padua", one day in Venice, one in Milan, would do very much to repair this gap it would after all do *something*; it was better, I argued, than re-maining in London not acquiring any knowledge of foreign places at all.

Richard Parker having sought and obtained more profitable employment I took with me as a secretary my old friend Barton Wills who was at first refused, by his TA Officer Commanding, permission 'to absent himself from the country in the present crisis' but afterwards persuaded the authorities to give grudg-ing consent. He had his own system of shorthand which would enable me to dictate throughout the journey—"Well, that was Siena; now let's get on with chapter five."

From the first it seemed to me that I was seeing the last of continental Europe for many years, perhaps for ever.

> Look thy last on all things lovely,
> Every hour — let no night
> Seal thy sense in deathly slumber
> Till to delight
> Thou hast paid thy utmost blessing;
> Since that all things thou wouldst praise
> Beauty took from those who loved them
> In other days.

Walter de la Mare's lines were in my mind and I noted with sympathy one of my fellow passengers, a lady of eighty-six whose daughter pluckily explained—"Mother may not have another chance to see all these interesting things if there is to be a war so we're going while we can."

And what remains of it all? Of the 'scenery' while in motion nothing at all. Of that coloured film running past the windows of the coach, rainswept or bright with May sunshine, sometimes mountainous but more often of level ground or mild slopes, I remember no detail and of the too lavish sightseeing only a few moments stand out. At Beauvais was a good hotel which has long since disappeared, its name, one would guess, making no appeal to the German invaders, the Hotel de France et de l'Angleterre. I made friends with several of the hotel staff and instead of chatting with my fellow passengers went with them to a café to play billiards on a continental table (no pockets) some skill on which I had acquired in Argentina. At Nice I won a tenner at roulette and at Rapallo had an early evening swim.

The Leaning Tower seemed to me very little more than an architectural freak and it has brought out the worst, the merely sightseeing side of people of all nations. Nearly every tourist attraction has something of beauty or atmosphere to recommend it, the Taj Mahal, Notre Dame, even the Tower of London. All that can be said of the campanile at Pisa is that it leans, and several million tourists a year come to see it leaning and buy little marble models to set up on the mantelpiece in Milwaukee or Millwall. It might have been a fine tower if the architects had not, out of ignorance or obstinacy, failed to correct its inclination while it was being built; as it is, it is the greatest tourist trap in the world. Imagine conversations dedicated to it.

"Have you seen the Leaning Tower of Pisa?"

"Yes."

"What do you think of it?"

There is no possible answer but that it leans, unless you are an engineer and grow technical.

I was not disillusioned when that char-à-banc emptied us out on the Campo Santo to stare at the thing and make the usual comments because I had a feeling before we came that it would not be my cup of tea. I do not like freaks in nature or art. I wanted to see the cathedral.

Florence was too much for me. It made me see the absurdity of this tour and of all organized sightseeing. I had been ready to jibe at this ever since I spent a summer in Stratford-on-Avon, but it was youthful, silly contempt for tourists as tourists, that superiority common to the sightseer all over the world who believes that everyone is a tourist except himself. But now I was hot with scorn, not for those who gaped at beauty but at those who exploited them. "One day's sightseeing in Florence" said the brochure. I knew this city was the richest in art of all Europe, that to the Uffizi Gallery alone a man could dedicate half a lifetime's contemplation of beauty, that the palaces of the great families of the Renascence, the Ricardi, Strozzi, Antinori and the rest, the Duomo and Giotto's campanile, the churches, museums, libraries, the great and little houses, had made Englishmen above all others adore Florence, turning it into a part of English literature. "One day's sightseeing . . ." I would have none of it. I sulked and walked about without a plan, had lunch at a small restaurant because I had seen *minestrone alla Fiorentina* on the menu, tried to pick up some sense of the place but because it happened to be a chilly and clouded day felt depressed and decided, with monstrous impertinence, that 'I did not like' Florence. I have never returned to it but still intend to spend an unbroken month at ease and alone in reparation.

I found, though, that I was enjoying the whole experience. I had felt self-conscious when first the coach had stopped at the portals of a hotel and we all alighted while our uniform suit cases were unloaded from the boot, but this had soon passed. I would not have chosen this means of progression, I would not have made a sightseeing tour at all at that point if I had not been invited to do so without expense, but I quickly lost my initial snobbishness about it, while at least I had the compensation of seeing everywhere the countless German tourists who since the formation of the Axis were coming to Italy for relief from the austere atmosphere of their country and to carry out their earnest researches armed with guide-books. The German tourist was far more distinguishable then than today and thought nothing of wearing a feather in his Tyrolean hat, carrying an alpenstock, taking photographs of his group posed against every piece of statuary he saw, wearing those fluffy highly patterned tweeds which his manufacturers alone in Europe turned out, stumping by in the heaviest of boots, even smoking hooked pipes and generally imitating foreign caricatures of himself, while Nazi badges appeared on his person, his luggage and his vehicles. At least, I consoled myself, our coachload of intelligent Midlanders did not look like these and when the octogenarian lady who might not have another chance hobbled along, greedy for more sightseeing, anxious to miss nothing on the way, I grew quite proud of her.

I resolved after Florence to take a middle way about sightseeing, dedicating some time to it but not rushing about determined, like the old lady, to omit no detail. I would choose one or two of the prospects offered in each place but recognized that I had not the background of knowledge or taste to do more than get an impression.

[2]

But Rome gave me more than that. Not much—what could Rome give to a not very well informed young man visiting her for the first time for a three days' stay?—but enough to remain in my mind, a reflection of clear brilliance, after thirty years.

It is when I think how little I know of Italy that I almost regret the love and knowledge I have of Spain, perhaps because to know Spain and its culture, history, literature is a

luxury for a civilized man, but to know Italy is an essential. The
Latin I had learned so laboriously, from the Caesar of my preparatory school to the Cicero and Juvenal of Tonbridge had
been kept alive in my mind by ecclesiastical Latin and something
remained of Catullus who spoke so intimately of life, of Pro-
pertius who exquisitely idealized it and Horace with his lyric
realism. Ovid and Virgil had never struck so deep in me and
though Martial was the sort of man I liked his epigrams were
too abstruse for my appreciation. I remember a sermon given
by the then Bishop of Stepney at Tonbridge School on the
text 'I see men as trees, walking' in which he promised us that
the splendour of the classics would be slowly revealed to us as
we laboured at Latin and Greek, at first as to the blind man
obscurely but later in their full glory. I had never got beyond
the stage of seeing men as trees walking but this was enough,
when I came to Rome, to make the remains of the ancient city
more populously alive than the plaster and statuary of the
nineteenth century or the architectural bombast of Mussolini.

The Colosseum, for instance. It took no feat of clairvoyance
to see that vast amphitheatre populated with a Roman crowd.
One could call them up as easily as a Hollywood producer with
a generous budget and hear them cheering the lions. But I
reached the Colosseum in the late afternoon when none but a
few stray sightseers were left and there was an uncanny silence
in the place which played on the imagination. There were no
pale and ancient ghosts here, tired by the centuries, but
swarthy and vivacious phantoms with the cruel savage stares
of wild animals.

But gentler spirits seemed to haunt the catacombs through
which we were led in a lingering crocodile by a guide. Of that
piece of sightseeing I have only one very clear recollection.
Dawdling behind my fellow tourists I looked into a small blind
side-passage and saw, behind a pile of stones and rubble, the
top part of a human skull. I picked it up and peered into its eye-
sockets. It was clean and white in no way like the skulls of
animals found in the fields in childhood, an ivory *memento mori*

such as grinned down on an alchemist in an old woodcut. I was about to conceal it under my arm when on a strong impulse, almost a command, I stooped and replaced it.

It was the improbability of the discovery that struck me most when I recalled it in the night—that a skull should lie undisturbed and unreclaimed two yards from where streams of tourists passed. But I did not regret having left it there. It would have been the souvenir to end all souvenirs, a skull from the Roman catacombs, but it might have been more than a souvenir, a relic; a sacred relic perhaps . . . But this speculation should stop. I was told to leave it there and I did.

St Peter's and the great *piazza* made me feel, as any man not intolerably arrogant must feel, a termite hastening about his insignificant business. But I was young enough also to know a juvenile and partisan pride in my Church, which had built the greatest dome in the world for the greatest temple. That it had been raised above the slums, that the men who had worked for a hundred and twenty years to build it lived in conditions of poverty, that it was paid for not only by the gold of emperors but by the pence of the penurious faithful, only increased its overpowering grandeur in my eyes.

After that I saw nothing, but for the last day wandered about the streets, sat in cafés, ate in a busy restauarant, as I was used to doing in any strange city. But at the hotel in which we had been booked to stay, the Flora in the Via Veneto near the Borghese gardens, I left my window open and was roused towards the morning by a thrilling chorus of countless nightingales which came flooding into the room till I gave up all thought of sleep and listened, delighted by this very classical sound. Good hackneyed quotations came into my head, till I was lilted towards sleep with Cory's

Still are thy pleasant voices, thy nightingales, awake;
For Death, he taketh all away, but them he cannot take.

What did it matter that Heraclitus lived in Ephesus and never came to Rome? It was all apiece with that dream, part of the classroom, part of reality, which is in the head of anyone who has learned at school of the Ancients.

[3]

We arrived in Naples in the afternoon of a windless May day and went to the Grand, a hotel overlooking the bay in the wide, promenade-like Via Caracciolo. My fellow passengers disappeared to their rooms to rest after the journey, to prepare themselves for dinner in the hotel dining-room or to sleep. Impossible for me—I left the hotel within five minutes of arrival and found waiting a few yards away the inevitable pimp. This seemed to me (at that lusty and irresponsible time) a good welcome to a city famous since Nero's time for the diversity of its vices, and I took a taxi at the man's suggestion to the Galeria. For two days I saw no more of European Motorways, or even of my friend Barton Wills, and I saw nothing of 'sights' or picture galleries, but a great deal of raw life in squalid and exciting places.

I had read somewhere that Naples was a Greek settlement, Neapolis, the new city as opposed to the long-vanished Palaeopolis, the old. Whether this was true or relevant I did not know but so powerful are words and legends that Neapolitans have always looked 'Greek' to me, belonging far more to the earlier Aegean tradition than the Guelphs and Ghibellines of the north, to the Mediterranean of Matthew Arnold

> As some grave Tyrian trader, from the sea,
>   Descried at sunrise an emerging prow
> Lifting the cool-hair'd creepers stealthily,
>   The fringes of a southward-facing brow
>   Among the Aegean isles;
> And saw the merry Grecian coaster come,
> Freighted with amber grapes, and Chian wine,
> Green bursting figs, and tunnies steep'd in brine;
>   And knew the intruders on his ancient home,

The young light-hearted Masters of the waves;
  And snatch'd his rudder, and shook out more sail,
And day and night held on indignantly
O'er the blue Midland waters with the gale,
    Betwixt the Syrtes and soft Sicily,
      To where the Atlantic raves
Outside the Western Straits, and unbent sails
    There, where down cloudy cliffs, through sheets
      of foam,
    Shy traffickers, the dark Iberians come;
      And on the beach undid his corded bales.

Perhaps this had no more foundation than that the people of southern Italy are on the whole darker than those of the north, more insinuating and humorous, more beautiful and more dishonest. I do not know. But I seemed to play with time during those two days, be somewhere in ancient history as well as in those narrow streets of tall dirty houses, or even further, in the dim underworld of pre-history. I did not sleep once at the Grand Hotel and except for one morning which I spent at Pompeii missed all the 'sights' and nearly missed the coach, too, when it left Naples.

The drive northwards is almost entirely lost to memory, like some of the mosaics of Pompeii, covered by rubble which has been accumulated in the intervening years. I remember Perugia in the hills, and how at the Brufani Palace, a hotel with a superb view, we were left waiting for food while German tourists were assiduously served. "I'm afraid we're not members of the Axis," said our courier, "but we're hungry all the same," on which the headwaiter smiled and diverted a couple of waiters from the Germans.

Assisi and Giotto's frescoes, melancholy beautiful Ravenna, Padua and a return to Venice, in which I had been fifteen months before on my way back from Eastern Europe. There is one among many peculiar qualities of Venice which attracts me—for all its waterways and palaces, its art and architecture, it is in some way a homely town: it loses its strangeness in a few days and grows comfortably familiar to visitors more quickly than any city I know, welcoming one back with a Sphinx-like and unchanging smile each time one arrives. Perhaps the absence of traffic and the changelessness of the architecture, perhaps the simple nature of the topography (though not of the native) made it—at least before the war—just as one left it a year, ten years ago, so that parents can bore their children by showing them the spot where they once did this or that on their honeymoon, and tourists can show photographs of themselves feeding the pigeons in the Piazza San Marco without fearing that a later visitor will say crushingly 'All that's been changed now.'

Yet Venice has changed in the last two decades, if not in appearance, in spirit. Had I realized it, in 1939 I was seeing the last of the Venice of Corvo, John Addington Symonds, Horatio Brown, and the rest, the English settlers who for a few pounds a year could hire something called a *palazzo* and live like doges in almost renaissance style. There were still private gondolas and strictly private gondoliers and though the river buses were already running the canals were leisurely and full of colour, the shops sold Venetian glass for less than it could be bought in London and the foreigner was not a profitable cross which had to be borne along with all the other tiresome features of post-war life, but an individual to be welcomed.

In Milan I had Italian friends and their conversation was more alarming than anything I had heard here before, and sharply brought me back from the past. Mussolini was *mad*, his head turned by all this nonsense about an empire and eight million bayonets. Only last month he wanted to show Hitler that *he* could grab countries, too, and had annexed Albania. Hadn't he started *racialism*—in Italy of all places? Fortunately no one took much notice of it—but the Grand Council had pushed through a law against Jews. No doubt about it, he would take the country into war. He would not listen to anybody. Mad. Bloodthirsty and mad.

It seemed as we drove up through France that the wind was rising behind us.

CHAPTER ELEVEN

Men and Women

IN London there seemed to be much public determination to behave as though nothing particular was happening, while air-raid wardens lecturing on the effects of poison gas, always explained that they were only taking precautions *in case* the worst came to the worst, adding brightly, "We hope it won't, don't we?"

It is in retrospect that we see that summer as clouded with terror, in retrospect that we were fatalistically aware of what was to come. In fact all but the most sage and farsighted* of us seized on any fragment of press optimism, any news item that seemed to suggest a good omen, and tried to turn over and go to sleep again. We could not, of course. The air was too oppressive, the clouds too low, but we did not abandon hope or the agreeable pursuits of life.

New acquaintanceships were touched with doom. I came to know three writers that summer all of whom, as it happened, I met again after the war, but at the time our meetings seemed like hurried introductions on leaving a ship after a voyage, too late to be fruitful. I met all three through the same genial intermediary who delighted in bringing together people who would interest, if not like one another. His name was Christopher Dilke and he was a grandson or grandnephew of one of the few interesting men in English politics since the end of the eighteenth century, Sir Charles Wentworth Dilke.†

---

*It is interesting to speculate on how those gloomy but all too truthful prophets would have reacted to peace if the generals' plot to exterminate Hitler had come five years earlier and been successful. Perhaps they would have foreseen that, too.

†Sir Charles Dilke's life-story has been written and filmed and depths of sentiment and romance have been mined and laid bare but he still does not figure in

Christopher Dilke in his early thirties had a maturity almost intimidating to me and succeeded in making me feel an enthusiastic youngster submitting ideas to his weightier judgment. He looked judicious, like a satisfied wine-taster at the end of a good season. He was a gourmet with a quite remarkable knowledge of food and wines and though he was now engaged to be married I fancied he had given the same speculative consideration to women as he gave to burgundy. He had read very widely; his taste in modern literature was esoteric but pronounced. Among Americans, for instance, he delighted in the work of William Faulkner, to me a precious and eccentric writer, and ignored such mainstream novelists as Sinclair Lewis. He did not look older than his years and he did not affect a premature ripeness yet I could not think of him as younger than I was.

There has survived, in a very slim packet of mnemonic items from before the war, a menu roughly painted in water-colours and scribbled in crayons, of a dinner given by Christopher and a friend named Yeatman with whom he shared a flat, an enchanting occasion which would have been memorable to me in essentials even without the card. Christopher and his friend were both skilled cooks and it does not seem to me in looking back that their calling themselves 'Jean' and 'Christophe' for the occasion was anything but the most aimiably youthful affectation. They are, for all I know, stern-minded barristers or commercial magnates now who would frown on this frivolous souvenir of their bachelor days, but I find poetry in it.

Il sera servi
le mercredi, le 3 mai
1939
aux invités les plus distingués
G. B. Stern
Miss Bond, Alice Best
et Rupert Croft-Cooke

---

the public mind as one of the more dramatic martyrs of Victorian puritanism, like Parnell or Richard Burton. But he was a far more remarkable man than either.

* le consommé mâitre jean
la fondue de Belley
le veau rôti
sce Bordelaise
la salade batarde
les canapés tria juncta
le café
* jean   * christophe
Chambéry
Chateauneuf
Pouilly Blanc Fumé

on the back of the card are our signatures, grinning at us from across the years.

I knew G. B. Stern to be one of that generation of women in literature who had earned for themselves the term woman novelist, or simply novelist, as distinct from 'lady-novelist' or 'authoress', names with which Mrs Humphrey Ward and Ouida had been perfectly content. Apart from Katherine Mansfield, Olive Shreiner and Virginia Woolf, who for one reason or another were detached from the main body, these writers knew and discussed one another and in the 1920s were all immensely successful figures to be revered by the young of both sexes. They were modern in the 1920s and 1930s, very much belonging to the literary world of Maugham, Walpole, Wells and Bennett, to a period when writers could afford to divide their time between London and the South of France with profitable visits to the United States occasionally. There was, as I found in later years, a great deal of Christian-name-dropping amongst them, and the identities of 'Hughie', 'Willie', 'Rebecca', 'Vita', 'Francis', 'H.G.' and 'Sheila' were to be instantly recognized on pain of being considered out of touch.

The women writers of whom I am thinking—they were not a 'school' in any sense and had no more in common than a belief in the novel—were May Sinclair, Clemence Dane, Rebecca West, Sheila Kaye-Smith and G. B. Stern, while Rose Macaulay was someone difficult and aloof and Dorothy Richardson a revered and impoverished country cousin to be aided when possible—or when her proud nature allowed it. Pamela Frankau and Marguerite Steen were later recruits in the same regiment.

G. B. Stern when she came into 'Jean and Christophe's' little flat that evening had an aura of success, acquaintance with the great and friendliness untouched by condescension. Like most of us who knew Louis Golding she went through periods of Not Speaking with him and this, she told me with some amusement, was one of them. From early days they had exchanged signed copies of their new books on publication and 'Peter' Stern had inadvertently sent Louis a copy of the American edition of one of hers thus, as Louis told me, 'slighting' him. "Can't she see that in any case since *Magnolia Street* it has become a very one-sided exchange? To send this when everyone knows that an author receives twice as many free copies of the American edition as of the English showed gross insensitivity." But we talked of him. Louis certainly had this, that when two or more people who knew him met they discussed him, usually with amusement, often with admiration, always with entertainment. We talked of other things, of Peter Stern's book *Little Red Horses*, a novel with the theme of a boy genius meeting a girl film star when they are being moved about the world by adults, we talked of wine and food and of *Wine and Food* for these were the days when André Simon's glorious little magazine was a family journal for epicures and spurned all vulgar and popular gimmicks, and we both said we liked one another and would meet again, a promise that was unfulfilled for ten years, and *those* ten years, to 1949, a lifetime.

Christopher also introduced me to a writer whose career I had more closely followed—Claude Houghton, one of those true novelists whose kind in the professional sense is dying out. There were writers before the war who without achieving vast sales had a sufficient reputation, a sufficient loyal readership to continue working in their genre, turning out a novel every year or two, maintaining a certain level of quality without achieving any book which could be hailed as a masterpiece (except in the sense that any new book to cause a momentary sensation was called a masterpiece by its publisher). Their sales-figures had their ups and downs, unrelated so far as they could see to the merits of their books, and the most profitable event in their lives was the sale of some film rights to Hollywood. Nowadays a novelist, known or unknown, may produce half a dozen books which fail to sell until his publisher tires of him, or he writes one timely book which booms and keeps him with its sidelines, radio, translation, serialization, television, dramatic rights, American lecture tours and the rest for several years. There is no middle way and the old-style professional novelist with a mildly discussed new book out every other autumn, a solid reputation and membership of the Savage Club must turn his hand to other work, writing copy for commercials perhaps, ghosting the memoirs of a famous politician or turning out children's books, if he wants to live.

Claude Houghton was not typical of these except perhaps in the circumstances of authorship—he was the most individual writer. I have tried before and countless critics have tried to convey the strange quality of suspense and mystery he achieved in a situation entirely psychological, how he could make one sweat to know what was so good, so evil, so fateful about Jonathan Scrivener or Julian Grant or Ivor Trent, what were the factors which held fate silent like a threatening thunderstorm over their heads. His secret, like that of one of the great prestidigitators, is gone with him to the grave for Claude Houghton died in 1961 and perhaps he himself never knew it. I read his books not reverently, for I recognized his as a minor talent however attractive, but avidly, greedy to know what the next page would reveal.

At lunch, when Christopher introduced us, he talked with rather pedantic enthusiasm about minor Jacobean playwrights whose work swam with gore. "Minor?" they both shouted indignantly when I used the word and it was plain that I had touched on the tender flesh of an obsession, or an affected obsession, with them both. Webster and his *Duchess of Malfi* and *The White Devil* might be very well, Kyd with his *Spanish Tragedy* was too much of a good thing.

"But Middleton?" they said triumphantly. "Haven't you read *The Changeling*?"

As it happened I had not and sulked accordingly, though not with any real ill-humour. I took a mischievous revenge on them by driving them, both nervous passengers, at speed from Soho to my flat, a drive which so scared Claude Houghton that he gave an account of it in one of his novels, calling the driver Rupert. But he was a gentle, friendly man of wide understanding as I found when I met him in after years. I had no more defence than any other young man not free from self-importance against skilled teasing.

The third writer to whom Christopher Dilke introduced me was John Marks. I write this less than a year after his death and I find it hard to convey anything of the personality of that unusual and likeable man. I say 'writer', and John was nothing *else* by profession but scarcely know if the title fits. He was nearer to genius than many whom one does not hesitate to call writers, yet he left behind him only one book, several times rewritten, on bullfighting and a few sheaves of articles and news items. He was paradoxical. His fault in worldly eyes was that he was too lazy to earn money by the only means he knew, writing, but never too lazy to write long, witty, sometimes digressive letters to his friends. He was too casual to keep the job of *The Times* correspondent in Spain, but never unpunctual or careless in doing some selfless kind act. Throughout his life, moreover, he was generous in the only way that really tests the impulses of modern man, with his time and his energy. And he was one of the best conversationalists I knew.

In 1939 he had not long abandoned that disastrous venture *Night and Day* and was returning to Spain very soon. He was an *aficionado* of the bullring not as English and American holiday-makers are today, full of boasts and the unnecessary use of Spanish terms in gesticulated descriptions, unable to tell a *torero* from a Cordobés. John knew. There was something occult in his sympathy with bullfighter and bull. His knowledge which was encyclopaedic was of secondary importance—it was that hypostatic understanding which made him later the greatest critic and historian of the bullring in any language.

My own knowledge was sketchy, gained at random from what fights I had been able to see, limited as I was by circumstances and impecuniousness. But at least I could talk with John.

"Why don't we make an anthology of bullfighting?" I suggested. I was always thinking up potential books at that time when the German Army was already on the Polish frontier.

John seized on the idea and for an hour or more we discussed it. Those who hated it should be included if they wrote well against it, Kipling's *The Bull that Thought* and E. V. Lucas's piece about a white horse. There was D. H. Lawrence's extraordinary passage about the bullring in Mexico City, and all the Frenchmen and of course Hemingway. We agreed that what would make it a good anthology was not so much the theme in itself but the fact that the theme had inspired, by sympathy and antipathy, some very fine writing.

John was enthusiastic and we decided to carry it further. But it lay dormant and forgotten till thirty years later. Meeting him in Madrid a few weeks before his death, I reminded John of it.

"Let's do it!" he said, the old enthusiasm lighting up. But he would never have done it if he had lived, never have got down to the details and research and if I ever turn to it, it will be as a memorial to John.

[2]

Dennis Wheatley was one of the very few writers I had met at Louis Golding's home, for Louis's friends were not usually drawn from among his fellow novelists, whom he suspected of being amused at him. Wheatley was then known as a writer of thrillers and whodunnits—not yet famous for black magic novels and such. He was enterprising and had invented a sort of cops and robbers game in which clues, such as a piece of fluff or a feather, were stitched into the pages of a folder—altogether the man to approach, I felt, with a scheme of my own.

This was a piece of naivety which should have been gently dismissed by Wheatley in a few moments' conversation. Myles Eadon in his capacity of free-lance had discovered something about a popular murder case which he believed was not known to the police, though looking back on it now I should think it unlikely that the facts, whatever they were, were not in possession of the CID men in charge of the case. I cannot, unfortunately, remember the details or what I thought I knew but I remember that a piece of evidence seeming as vital as one of Wheatley's specimens of dust was in my possession.

I had published a whodunnit under a pseudonym and my plan was that two or three writers of detective novels should show that their talents were not limited to describing mysterious crimes in fiction but that they could actually solve one by their literary detectives' methods in real life.

I telephoned Wheatley and he asked me to come and talk to him about it that evening. With unmannerly enthusiasm I drove off in the Opel at once, arriving before the poor man and his family had finished dinner. I told him my scheme, and all I had to back it, except The Clue, which I intended to keep until the plan to investigate had gone a step further. Wheatley appeared interested but was quite non-commital. However, he temporized and told me in the friendliest way that I should have to convince 'a third party' before he was prepared to consider it. Some time later 'the third party' appeared.

I was not very shrewd or worldly in the matter of character. I trusted far less than today in my own reading of physiognomy. But every instinct I had told me that the man who entered the room was a cad and a potential con man. It was Peter Cheyney.

I once mentioned Cheyney's name to Compton Mackenzie who replied quite seriously—"What I suspect of Peter Cheyney is so heinous that I don't want to tell you, in case it's untrue."

Pressed, because I could not bear to be left with something as tantalizing as that, he said—"I have reason to think he was in the Black and Tans." As Cheyney made no secret of this there was no need for such discretion.

Dennis Wheatley, a man of breeding and principle, must have been made extremely uncomfortable by what followed. Cheyney took the floor and for half an hour practised the sort of interrogation he had learned to use on some unfortunate IRA man. I had the feeling that if we had not been in Wheatley's house he would have tried more violent methods of making prisoners talk. What *was* my clue? How did I expect him to judge the possibilities of the situation without knowing? Didn't I realize the seriousness of this? If I really knew something which I had not reported I might well be charged with complicity. That would mean prison. How could I seek to involve others? Come on now, what *was* the clue? Finally he did not believe I had one. It was bluff. I was looking for cheap advertisement at Wheatley's expense.

I formed two resolutions during this interrogation. One was that in no circumstances would I reveal what I knew. The other that I would never speak to this overbearing cheapjack of literature again. I kept both.

[3]

But there were pleasanter people to know in that year of varied acquaintances and better things to do than to think out plans for publicized criminology. That year, for the only time, I did what so many successful novelists of the period did frequently, I bought a modern painting.

I knew Clifford Hall as a painter who for some years chose chiefly circus subjects and was to be met 'round the back' at Olympia in winter. But as I came to see more of his work I understood, or thought I understood, that the circus was incidental to the purpose in many of his pictures, to catch one motionless moment in activity, not to paint movement but to make his theme instinct with movement. So the ballet, circus, theatre gave him scope for pictures which were brilliantly decorative but more than that had an immense vitality of their own. He loved the sea, and in an exhibition of his paintings which is open as I write* there is one which exactly interprets this, two male figures seen only in outline from behind with hands in pockets look out over a glassy sea from the water's edge, pausing a moment from an idle walk along the line of surf. Only in the famous *Danseuse sur la Scène* of Degas had I seen this one motionless second in a swirl of action caught so perfectly as Clifford could catch it in his pictures of acrobats and ballet dancers and it was this which attracted me in his work.

A modest, unassertive man who in appearance resembled Joseph Conrad, he asked me to come down to his Chelsea studio in an old rat-run of a house built for artists in the nineteenth century. As any purchaser should, I scarcely saw anything but the painting I wanted—that of a young ballet dancer in practice dress leaning against the rail of a rehearsal room. It represents a discontinuity, no more, in the dancer's movements; in the briefest of seconds he will be gone and the wall remain blank where his blue shirt had made a shadow.

I had been collecting early English water-colours for fifteen years and had been successful in finding them in places where their value was not appreciated. But I had not expected to be able to acquire the work of a living man. Moreover, I met the model young Leo Kersley of the Ballet Rambert who had in life just that proneness to sudden movement and perched ready to be off where others would sit or stand. The painting gave me a new kind of possessiveness when it was hung in the entrance hall to the flat just two months before the outbreak of war in which that flat (though not my possessions) was destroyed. It survived enemy bombing but I was to lose it through more squalid means; it was sold to meet the expense of that unassuagable monster called Legal Costs in 1953.

*Clifford Hall Paintings of the Seaside, 1934–66. Anthony d'Offay Fine Art.

CHAPTER TWELVE

Out of London

WHEN the Spanish Civil War ended in March I felt relief, more than anything else, that the bloodshed was over. My interest had never been a political one. Most of my contemporaries seemed desperately anxious that one side or the other should 'win', and despised non-intervention not because it was an attempt to limit the war (however unsuccessful and misdirected) but because it favoured Franco. I had loved Spain since adolescence, not Republican Spain or Fascist Spain, but the country, the people, the spirit and throughout the war I had imagined or read of the outrages and longed for an end of the daily reports of new massacres and inhumanities. In this I had found myself, surprisingly as it seemed to me then, alone among my acquaintances who wanted arms for Spain.

That summer, when the war was over and the leaders of the various parties which had fought together and among themselves on the Republican side were quarrelling abroad, each disclaiming his blameworthiness for defeat, while half a million refugees were existing in unspeakable conditions on the French side of the frontier, I was asked by Peter Davies to translate an account of the final struggle in Madrid written in Spanish by Colonel Segismundo Casado. I read the manuscript and decided that I could do this with a good heart.

Hugh Thomas, whose book *The Spanish Civil War* is for the most part an honest and painstaking work on a subject still confused by passion and propaganda, is less than fair to Casado. He does not so much misstate the facts as by small malicious embroideries reveal his prejudice, or that of Alvarez del Vayo by whom he seems to have been influenced. For instance "Due to telegraph delays (attributed by Azcarate and Alvarez del Vayo to the wilful interference by Colonel Casado) Negrin's affirmative reply did not reach Paris until Feb. 25". " 'Only we Generals can get Spain out of war' said Casado, who had already given orders for his new insignia as a General to be placed on his uniform." "The colonel (he had now dropped his General's rank for fear that it might prejudice his relations with Franco)." "Casado allowed himself, after a show of modesty, to be named President of the future Nationalist Council." "By his action he had ruined the possibility of any further Republican resistance." (This is particularly disingenuous, written as it is of the situation less than a week before surrender.)

In fact Casado was one of the few leaders to come out of that tragic and in many ways squalid conflict with clean hands. Imagine his situation in February and March 1939. A professional soldier without political affiliations he had remained loyal not to any party but to the government of his country, conceiving it his duty to put down rebellion however it occurred. He was now forty-six years old and after the fall of Catalonia, Commander of the Army of the Centre, the only force defending Madrid against the encirclement, complete except for the ports of Valencia and Alicante, by Franco's now well-equipped and organized army. He had less than 40 aircraft and many of them not in flying condition. His total armament consisted of 95,000 rifles, 1600 machine-gun rifles, 1400 machine-guns, 150 pieces of artillery, 50 mortars and 10 tanks, while many of his men were without boots or overcoats. Nearly all the political leaders had fled to France, Azaña the President of the Republic, Aguirre President of the Basque Republic, Luis Companys President of Catalonia, and Largo Caballero the Socialist leader, among them; Azaña twice refused to return to Spain when deputations implored him and eventually (on February 28) resigned the Presidency.

France and Britain had recognized Franco's regime and what remained of the Republican fleet had been bombed out of

Cartagena and remained uselessly at sea till it reached Bizerta and was interned by the French. Madrid, always arctically cold in February, was without fuel and almost without food. There was virtually no civilian transport, no hot water, medicine or surgical supplies.

Negrín, the Prime Minister, who remained in his house at Yeste near Valencia and issued hysterical orders to resist and go on resisting, sent for Casado and gave him promises of faery gold. There were 10,000 machine-guns, 600 aircraft and 500 pieces of artillery sent by Russia waiting at Marseilles, he said, and after promoting Casado to General sent him back to continue that futile resistance from Madrid. When the soldier realized that the politician's promises were empty and that Negrín himself was planning to abandon Spain he did, as Mr Thomas not very frankly reports, remove his insignia and revert to his former rank. He also told Negrín that he would no longer accept his orders but had formed a National Council of Defence with the intention of surrendering Madrid on the best terms obtainable. Negrín left by plane for France.

Casado then had to put down a Communist rising in the city and for six days there was heavy fighting while Franco's armies prepared for their triumphal entry. Small wonder that the terms of surrender which Casado obtained were not lavish, but it was not quite unconditional surrender and the lives and property of many thousands of people were saved before Casado himself went down to Valencia with the members of his Defence Council and embarked on a British ship.

Since then he had been in London writing his book—*Los Ultimos Días de Madrid*. But news values change and the war with which we had all been so vitally concerned a few months earlier had been pushed from our memories before the end of summer, perhaps by a sense of guilt or perhaps because of the greater threat to peace. Casado had not found it easy to get a publisher and perhaps Peter Davies, who was a godson of J. M. Barrie and said to be the original of Peter Pan, felt it a duty to history. It was written with the accuracy and attention to detail of a military commander's report and was dry and unemotional.

I met Casado only once, memorably, for a few hours. He had the disarming quality of outright frankness. He answered my questions patiently and dispassionately. He was very much a professional soldier, very Spanish, and one found it difficult to imagine him deciding historical events. I liked him and trusted him, but I did not make a very good job of the translation of his book.

For one thing, I had only three weeks in which to complete it, since both publisher and author wanted to bring it out before all issues of the Spanish war would have passed from the fickle memory of readers. I decided to leave London and went down to Beckley in Sussex with an Irish shorthand typist and an inadequate dictionary to work on it.

Beckley, and its pub the Royal Oak and its publican Charlie Goddard, I had discovered for myself when walking through Sussex as a boy of eighteen and it had been a refuge for me at intervals ever since. I could always sleep in the four-poster bed and sit before the giant open fireplace in the room behind the bar. But this time, impelled by a boyhood memory of fishing from Hastings pier, I bought a rod and waited for a tinkle from some unfortunate dab while I dictated *The Last Days of Madrid*, perhaps hardly the most conscientious way of catching the last nuance of meaning in the original. Not that there were many nuances in that serious report. But I think now I showed extraordinary lack of imagination in treating the life-work of a man, the apology on which his place in history depended, with so little concentration and care. However, it remains, of necessity, one of the source books on the Spanish Civil War, as Mr Hugh Thomas's last chapters distinctly show.

[2]

In London during July I became aware of public tension.

Perhaps it was the warm pacific weather which made people imagine the sky full of bombers and buildings toppling into the street as they did in Hollywood earthquakes, reproduced by means of models. I remember one breathless evening walking in Hyde Park with Dingo, feeling the benevolent English summer at its kindest. A military band was playing near the statue of Achilles and the crowd round it overflowed from the deck-chair circle to the grass, listening to Sullivan or Strauss, lazily chatting, apparently at peace. But it was not peace. This summer was not like any other which brought strollers to the park at night. The band, the fading sunlight, the dried grass were not reassuring pleasant things, welcome to Londoners out of stuffy homes, but privileges seized while there was yet time, precarious pleasures which might soon be lost for ever. I daresay the crowd round the bandstand did not talk of war, did not threaten one another with that immemorial prediction— "As soon as the harvest's in. That's all they're waiting for," but in everybody's mind there was foreboding.

We did not discuss European politics intelligently. Those of us who still Hoped had small reason for hoping and those who Knew were not much more logical. But there was a sort of instinctive huddling together, that summer, as of a threatened flock, and odd little demonstrations of it which we would not for a moment admit. Where the National Anthem, played at the end of a cinema show, was used to produce nothing but a grabbing of personal belongings and a struggle to reach the doors, there was now a good deal of self-conscious standing, not stiffly to attention but in stern disapproval of those who had no patience with such conventions. Attendance at Church of England services at which prayers for the Royal Family and for peace were read (so it was reported in the press) increased by nearly fifty per cent.

I do not believe that anybody's attitude to events in 1939 was an entirely consistent one. We all veered and swayed on the lightest impulse. But as Poland was threatened it became more hardset. The Government had named a point beyond which we would not go in appeasement and most of us accepted it. This meant a fatalism, which we called resolve, very different from the vacillations of Munich.

But it did not mean despair, or even defeatism. "If it comes, it comes," we said and "We shall have to get it over with, I suppose." If we tried to visualize the form war would take we saw something like the trenches of Flanders in 1914-18. Yet there was still a hope, just a hope, that it would not come.

[3]

I can offer no satisfactory explanation for my activities during that fateful month because I have only a sporadic memory of my own emotions and motives then or at any time. I bought a light trailer caravan because I had planned to join the Rosaires in August for the back end of their tenting season, but whether I did so in defiance of fate, or because I did not believe the war, if it came, would immediately involve me or the Rosaires, I do not remember. It may have been because the only sane way to proceed was according to plans already made—we had had nearly two years of threats from Hitler already—or it may have been (though this is unlikely) that I thought a trailer caravan might be useful in wartime.

I certainly wanted to get out of London and be back in the reassuring countryside. This was not yet fear, though I should later know a particular fear of being in a great city bombed from the air. It was a longing for the surroundings in which I had been reared. Cities were man made and could be destroyed by man, but woods and fields were indestructible, overgrowing the ancient cities laid waste.

Moreover the Rosaires were in Sussex, moving eastward into Kent, so I should be in the counties I knew best.

I had no premonition, when I left the flat, that I should never sleep in it again. Myles Eadon was in camp with his Territorial unit and would return to it shortly, so it was left untouched. But had I realized it, I was leaving for ever the London I had known since childhood, in which the changes had come so slowly that I was unaware of them. I would see London again, briefly on leave in the black-out of 1941, and return to live in a different city in 1946.

I had come to London less than two years before in the belief, not uncommon to provincials, that it would lead to worldly success. If that was seriously my object I had failed. I had met a great number of people who interested me, gone abroad whenever I had a chance, written for a variety of papers and seen my name frequently in print, but of material success as the masters measured it I had achieved very little and of social success none at all. I had not secured a place at the luncheon table of Sybil Colefax or Emerald Cunard, redoubtable *salonnières* of the time, or even at the fireside of Eddie Marsh, resolute collector of young writers. Nor, at the other extreme, had I become a contributor to *New Writing* or been approved by John Lehmann and his circle. But those two years had been very precious and of all the homes I have left behind after a year or two there is none with happier memories than the low-ceilinged flat in Upper Berkeley Street. It was destroyed by bombs and the site was replanned so that it was not occupied after that Saturday morning when I drove cheerfully away to find the circus.

[4]

This was more than escapism, it was escape. The Rosaires like other nomads in England did not think about war. Unversed in politics, they had a refreshing attitude of incredulity towards such imbecilities. People who lived in houses, they seemed to say, were capable of some quite illogical behaviour but not, surely, such flagrant lunacy as a second world war. They were intelligent but not intellectual and were immersed in their day-to-day life which left them little time for reading newspapers or listening to news bulletins. Then again, theirs was a cosmopolitan profession; the vocabulary used by circus people is compounded of words drawn from German, Italian, Romanes, Hindustani and Spanish and they were accustomed to associate with artists of all nations. They had not, therefore, the English prejudice, commoner at that time than now, against foreigners among whom almost anything was rather more than likely to happen. Their view was sane, but alas, the view of a minority in any country. They were, of course, as vulnerable as the rest of us, but they remained unaware of danger till it came and to spend the last month of peace with them after all the harrowing uncertainties of London may have been self-deluding but it was refreshing, too.

I joined them at Liphook, having driven through the Hindhead country to find them just over the Surrey border. There was always something crab-like and side-faced about their welcome. They would affect not to have seen one for a while, then suddenly burst into greeting, or pretend to be keenly displeased or surprised at one's arrival before they expressed any welcome. But soon the old routine would be resumed; I would find myself drinking tea in one or another of the waggons, seeing performance after performance, wandering round the *tober* day-long, making coffee at midnight for anyone who came in from the August starlight to sit in my trailer talking for an hour, forgetting the few hours of sleep that were left before an early start.

From Liphook we drove in the pale gold of dawning sunlight to Havant, where we should stay for the week-end. Our *tober* was providentially off the main road, but a quarter of a mile away from it the August Sunday procession of cars and bicycles was speeding in a continuous stream to Hayling Island, and over the ferry the island itself was lively with fun fairs and char-à-bancs, ice-cream vendors, photographers, holiday camps and car parks. It was a typical English resort on a typical

English Sunday, and no one seemed to feel the smallest threat.

That Monday, I remember, Dennis (the wirewalker) told me that he had put something new into his act, and I went in to the afternoon show to find that as a last trick he had a plank handed up to him, and balancing it on the wire he spread his legs wider and wider till a foot had approached each end of the board. It was difficult and effective, and was discussed with a strange seriousness by the tent-men and grooms, to whom any small innovation or change in the show seemed always to be a matter of moment. It had been a hot day, so hot that the interior of the tent, which in summer was always filled with scent of growing grass suddenly made pungent by enclosure under a canvas roof, had been hard to bear for the performers, and they had gone to their waggons, perspiring. It was still broad daylight when a party of us went down to the nearest inn before the night show, but it was a little cooler. We drank our beer gratefully.

I watched, as I was never tired of watching during our travels, the attitude of the local customers to us. They always knew who we were—'chaps from the circus'—and they always showed sidelong curiosity. They good-humouredly tried to get the boys to talk and dropped other conversation while we were there, but they never quite accepted us. We were usually rather unkempt, for the boys took delight on working days in wearing the most miscellaneous clothes. We never deliberately monopolized the tap-room but very little seemed to be said or done there while we stayed.

Back on the circus field we heard that there had been some trouble at the paybox in which the Countess issued tickets. But one of the boys had been at hand and it was all over now. Perhaps the Rosaires were a little aggressive in looking after their property. They had learnt to protect their own, not as householders and factory-owners with all the paraphernalia of modern civic life, police and telephones, burglar-alarms, theft-proof safes and insurance, but by the simple exercise of their natural strength and intelligence. It seemed to me, as I watched the Countess pack up her little tin cash-box before taking it across to her waggon, that this respect of a man for what he owns, this determination to guard it and increase it, was a virile thing. It has no suggestion of miserliness but shows a man's determination to protect not only his person from insult but his property from interference.

The show had started, and I knew from the music that Martin Russell Hawkes was showing his lions. I was alone in front of the big tent, for the audience were all in and the Countess had gone back to her waggon. The sunset had faded now——there was only a lemon tinge to some reefs of slate-coloured cloud, and darkness was fast getting the better of that. I knew every note of the facile tunes the band played, knew just where the lions would be crouching, at what point Martin would be throwing his whip aside and lying full-length beside his creatures, I could hear Derrick in the band, for his passion for trumpet-playing made him slip in among the musicians every night till he was due to perform in the ring. Away on the road the cars were still streaming back from Hayling Island, but Havant itself was more or less in peace and the audience in the tent remained for the tense climax of Martin's act, quiet and breathless.

If this could only continue, I thought, this happy curriculum of travelling through the rich August days, of seeing the circus programme again and again, each performance subtly different from the others, of easy friendship with these unusual people. I have wanted at many points in my life to arrest progress there and then, to hold up a policeman's hand to growth and alteration, but never, I think, more heartily than I wanted it that evening, with the beaded electric-light bulbs of our tent-front blurred against the sky and the thumping brass band playing for the lion-trainer's finale.

Martin strolled out of the tent, his act finished, to supervise the removal of his lions in their little cage-fronted waggon to their places in the zoo. He shouted something to me, and gave a helping push as the tent-men started to tug that heavy cart. Then he wandered off to his own waggon to change. It was only after he had gone that one of the men told me, "Martin got a scratch tonight."

That, I knew, might mean anything. It could conceivably be taken literally, or it could refer to a serious wound. No lion-trainer has ever worked long without some marks of his calling. In Martin's waggon I found Ida Rosaire, to whom Martin was now engaged to be married, binding up a pretty deep wound down the fleshy offside of his hand. They were both outwardly very casual about the scratch, Martin because he felt casual, Ida because she had courage enough to be the future wife of a short-sighted lion-trainer.

"I think," said Martin reflectively as the bandaging was finished, "I shall have the two cubs in the act tomorrow. I've been meaning for a long time to show the five together." He began to unwind his khaki puttees.

Back in the big tent I found that Ivor was showing the new elephant—Princess Monice. He had worked during the winter to teach her a number of tricks, for she had come from a zoo where her only performance had been the monotonous one of carrying children up and down. She was the happiest elephant living, as meek and sentimental as a model schoolgirl, yet so powerful that when one of the laden lorries was stuck in the mud she pressed her great forehead against it and stepped forward slowly, pushing the whole thing before her. She was capable of a kind of tearful shame if she were spoken to harshly, and took pleasure in doing whatever she was asked. Ivor showed her admirably, for the two were the greatest friends. The act seemed almost a flirtation between them.

Then Vivienne, after performing on the trapeze, came and joined her mother and me in the seats just inside the entrance, vivacious and happy because it had been a sunny day, because it would be so again tomorrow, because her exquisite brief performance had been more successful than usual tonight, because she was young, she was Vivienne, she had always the wakeful inexhaustible happiness natural to her, instead of the moody almost guilty happiness of more lethargic or more intellectual women. Presently Dennis joined us, and we chatted intermittently of the show as it proceeded, of the tour and of future tours, of those who were performing and of other performers, but not of war. War that evening was remote.

Then as the show ended and the audience began to leave the tent gossiping cheerfully because they had enjoyed themselves, the tent-men had already begun to pull down the wallings, for the sooner the big tent was down and packed away the sooner they could sleep. Most of the audience moved towards the zoo where Charlie Lawrence was standing in his little open pay-box shouting lustily that they were just in time to see the lions fed. But presently the zoo was empty and its lights extinguished, the fronts of the lions' and bears' cages set in position for the night, and what had been a small enclosure behind an illuminated front became two lorries and two trailers, ready to move in the morning.

The *tober* was deserted now, save for our own people. The tent-men were singing as they pulled down, their voices travelling across the dark and empty field like the voices of water-men. Now that our strings of electric lights were out one became conscious of the white fire of stars over us, and a sickle moon untouched by clouds. The village, too, was at rest, the doors of our waggons were shut, and only the tent-men's song broke silence.

But suddenly the song stopped and from the far side of the field came laughter—loud rather wild laughter and a few shouts of protest. One of the men as he passed me said that Jimmy Parsons, who was tent-master that year, was losing his trousers. This was true enough, for a moment later Jimmy appeared in his shirt, his bare feet in the cold dew and a cigarette still lighted in his lips, to borrow a pair of grey flannels. His had been considered so disreputable that they had been confiscated. Jimmy, who had once known all the immaculate precision of a tailor's assistant, was wholly unperturbed.

Whence, I wondered, did they draw their energy? After half the work they had done most human beings would be carrying out their tasks in a state of fatigued stupor. But they found the breath and muscle left for horseplay half and hour before midnight when they had worked without much intermittence since daybreak.

At last, however, the lorries were packed ready, and they had wandered away to rest. All that remained of our huge white canopy was a group of stacked vans. It was quiet enough to hear the horses munching. There was a last call of good night as a door slammed, then the last light in a waggon window was extinguished and there was silence.

This was an immense moment for me. I was back with the circus, privileged to belong to it, accepted, free from preoccupation, utterly content. There would be many tomorrows as splendid as this. As sure as the sun would rise our waggons would move on. What nonsense was this of Poland and Hitler and another war?

CHAPTER THIRTEEN

The Last of Bosie

IT is difficult to resist a novelist's temptation to see the circus progressing through those Sussex villages under a cloud of doom which would eventually burst in tragedy, because in a sense that is what it was doing, going on to a certain fateful point in its journey where war would be declared and its progress ended. But this would be a literary device conceived in retrospect. The Rosaires were unconscious of anything impending which they could not meet and overcome as they had overcome so many near-insuperable checks to their progress and I was willing enough to share the sense of security which self-reliance so absolute had given them.

But they were more vulnerable than in previous years because their show was larger. They had purchased a new big tent that winter which made them, in seating capacity, the third largest tenting show in Great Britain, and they had spent capital on Princess Monice their magnificent elephant. They employed other turns and had a large staff of tent-men and bandsmen while their daily food bills for the animals were considerable.

When the tent was up, the flags out and the band playing the circus made a brave show. We went to Emsworth from Havant and stood on a large open field which sloped upwards slightly from the gate by which we had entered. This meant that the ornamental front of the show, with its giant sign of 'Rosaire's Circus' formed by two long signboards hinged on the tops of two waggons drawn up in front of the tent, had a more imposing look than usual, and our own trailers and waggons formed an avenue up from the entrance of the field. The grass was dry,

almost scorched, the sun was again in full blaze, and at noon we
were stretched on the ground basking lazily while the wireless
in the Countess's waggon played distantly. German soldiers,
I suppose, were taking their last Polish lessons or were already
on troop trains leaving for the frontier. Yet of Emsworth I
remember best that it was from here that Princess Monice left
us with Ivor to take part in a Sabu film at Denham.

From there we went to Chichester, arriving unfortunately on
market day—unfortunately, because it is a bad day for a circus,
and we had looked to Chichester, a prosperous little town, to
give us a packed house. Our *tober* was only a few hundred yards
from the Market Cross, but the audience was a small one.
Driving to Petworth the next morning I passed the Count with
the monkey-cart and his little cavalcade of ponies, and beside
him on his box-seat sat Ruth Manning-Sanders who had
joined the show on the previous day. She always drove with
the count in the morning when she was with us, loving the
trot of the horses, the fresh smell of the air which is lost to
motorists, and the journey made longer. With a scarf round her
head, she would sit there chatting with the Count, waving to
the successive lorries, waggons and cars as they passed.

Petworth, as I remember it from that visit was a place of tea-
shops and antique shops owing their prosperity to visitors to
Petsworth Manor, but I have never seen that treasury of
Grinling Gibbons carvings and pictures, because travelling
with a circus means just that and no more. Things that might
have interested me if I had come casually and alone were oddly
irrelevant now. I was concerned with the crowd we should
draw and scarcely left the *tober* which was half a mile from the
village on the fork of two main roads.

We drove on next day through the wooded country of west
Sussex to Billingshurst, a village which until half a century ago
must have had, more than most Sussex villages, an independent
life of its own. It was cheerful but unprofitable, though
Pulborough was more rewarding. Here we stood on a ground
which stretched right down to the river's edge. When the big

tent was up the water seemed to flow in a winding current right round it. Some of the tent-men bathed, but not the Rosaires, who find that even a short swim is apt to make their acrobatic work harder and less sure. Over our reed-circled ground was another cloudless sky, and Sussex seemed to be boasting of her peace and plentitude. All the afternoon I lay down by the water's edge, too lazy and too happy even to see the afternoon show.

We reached Arundel on Sunday morning, just a fortnight before the declaration of war. We were on level ground below the town and the castle stood over us on the hill. We went to hear mass in the great Catholic church built by one of the dukes of Norfolk in the last century and our party came out marvelling at the singing. On our way back to the *tober* we were held up by the march past of eight thousand Territorials on their way back from camp—just nine months before many of them must have been killed in the weeks preceding Dunkirk and on the beaches.

Still the sky remained cloudless, and Steyning gave us two good houses. When we reached Henfield next morning it was the hottest day of the whole summer, and the great trees beyond the common on which we built up were loud with the contented cooing of pigeons, and the common itself, which must have been the setting for many fairs and circuses in the past, made a perfect *tober*. The big tent standing among the gorse bushes, the lion-waggon on the open ground with children walking across from the road to listen to the beasts they could not see, the tent-men lying in the shadow of a living-waggon when the tent was up, everyone sunburnt, lazy and thirsty, the air so still that the flag on the big pole hung idly—it was the most placid picture. But at eleven o'clock I bought a newspaper, and read that Germany had signed a non-aggression pact with Russia.

[2]

I remember precisely my reaction to that. It was not resentment, surprise or fear. It was a realization of the futility of all speculation, of all reasoned hope, of all attempts to desire this or that to happen. There were incomprehensible powers and issues and I who had believed myself reasonably well informed, who had been looked to by my friends for an opinion, would never again suppose that I was more than a blind unit among so many. Somewhere, out of the ken of all reasoning beings, in some Kafkaesque stronghold beyond human discovery, omnipotent beings or demoniac spirits played with frontiers, alliances, loyalties, patriotism, staking them like stocks and shares and smiling over the ironies of war. What use was there in thinking, waiting on events, hoping, planning, resolving? Henceforward I would believe in Them. If there was a war and I had to join the forces it would be as a private soldier. I would no longer try to control my life.

But this news broke the impassivity even of the Rosaires. It was no longer possible to keep up a pretence of indifference. It was coming, now. An army lorry driven past the common which an hour ago would have had no more significance than a baker's delivery-van, became a threat and a portent, and a group of Territorials in the local public house became fateful young men, instead of town workers who spent a fortnight a year in uniform. The balloon, as one of the tent-men said, was about to go up. Our idly grazing horses and sleepy bears, our hot waggons and grass-scented tent, we ourselves were threatened with extinction.

Still the afternoon show was crowded, and when we moved on to Horsham on Friday we were more perturbed by the inaccessibility of the ground booked for us than by the Russo-German Pact. It was too far out of town and separated from the main road by a secluded lane.

"A nice quiet place," said Derrick ironically. "We're

not likely to be disturbed by any *people* coming up here."

He was only too right, and this was serious for they were showing for two days here. But the family, in spite of the poor season behind them and the acute uncertainty of the future, accepted their bad luck very philosophically. They were glad of a day on which they did not have to build up, and could lounge about during the morning, or go up to the town to do some of the shopping for which they had lacked time and opportunity so long.

On the Sunday morning—the last Sunday, as it transpired, of peace-time —we came to Crawley. The weather continued in the settled splendour of August, and the few strolling people who watched our long caravanserai move into its appointed field wore flannels and moved apathetically. Just before the afternoon show on the Monday Lord George Sanger, grandson of the founder of the Sangers and now in his eighties, came on the field. In spite of my association with the Rosaires I had met few of the great personalities of the past and this one's circus life stretched back into Victorian times. He lived not far away, now that he had retired from the circus business, and a show in the district was sufficient to bring him over. He knew all the Rosaires, of course, had seen the younger generation grow up from child performers, and spoke warmly to me of the family. But the history of his own show went back further.

"It started through the press-gang," he told me, as he sat stretched in a deck-chair near the Countess's waggon, waiting for the performance to begin. This seemed a little disconnected, but he explained it.

"My grandfather and his brother had come up to London in the time of the Napoleonic wars," he said, "when on their very first afternoon in the city there was a press-gang alarm, and they had to run for their lives. My great-uncle got away by being given refuge under the counter of a chemist's shop. He got work there afterwards and later started the firm of city chemists which is still called Sanger's, I believe. But they caught my grandfather and he did ten years in the navy, and lost one eye and three fingers. There were no proper pensions then, but sailors who had fought for their country were rewarded with a lump sum of money, and a licence permitting them to start a public house or a place of public performance. When my grandfather came out he met a man who persuaded him to start a circus, and that's how he began. I had more than fifty years of it—but the next generation seems to be going out of the business. Yes, I suppose it's a pity, but they're doing well in other things. This is a hard life, you know.

"If you'd come on my show and asked for Mr Sanger you'd have been told there wasn't such a man. It was a rule I made, and saved me no end of trouble. But it nearly cut both ways once when a man I'd never seen came up to me and asked if I was Mr Sanger. 'No,' I said. 'There no such person here.' But later he found out I really was, and told me his name was Bertram Mills, and that he'd rented Olympia for the whole winter. He booked up all our elephants. That winter was the beginning of Bertram Mills's Circus . . ."

Someone came across to tell us that the show was just beginning, and the old man rose briskly. He did not mean to miss the first act. But then no circus man does—of any other circus. In this closed world whatever invidiousness or even jealousy there may be, whatever personal enmities or rivalries, there is great generosity, great appreciation, great gusto in the game itself. No one applauds a good act harder than another circus man who happens to be in the audience.

Forest Row, to which we came on Tuesday to stay for two days, was openly suffering from what was still called—though no longer contemptuously—'war scare'. Ivor and Derrick Rosaire, who had been in Germany with me and had been treated with the usual emotional kindness of the Germans, remained sceptical. But the rest, and the tent-men, had already begun to discuss what they would do when the thing started. Still the weather was torrid, the countryside flamboyant. Still the affairs of the circus seemed of paramount importance, and an unexpectedly good house for the evening show at Forest Row put everyone in a good temper.

Ivor had brought Princess Monice from Denham, her grey and bristly hide still coloured by some pink pigment that had been painted on it for the purposes of filming. Chris, the groom, a tough old soldier, understood and loved her. He had slept in her shed all through the previous winter, and used to talk to Monice like a child. Ivor, who showed her in the ring, was more authoritative with her, but no less appreciative of her gentle good nature. She appeared in the ring immediately and there were jokes about seeing pink elephants. So our own affairs absorbed us still.

On Wednesday I drove the Count to see his advance agent, and discuss the future route. At Lewes, where we should be tomorrow, we found his trail, and knew that we must go on to seek him at Newhaven. The Sussex county town seemed placid and commonplace enough, and the *tober* we should occupy tomorrow just outside the prison walls, looked promising. In a low-ceilinged public house we fell into conversation with a few of the customers, who were far more interested in the prospect of a circus tomorrow than of a war next week.

"It's all another bluff," a beefy farmer asserted. "But this time we've called it. He'*ll* never go into Poland. He wouldn't have touched Czechoslovakia either if we'd had the sense to do what were doing now. By this time next week we shall be laughing over this scare."

The town was its usual busy self, the prosperous shops crowded, the doors of the banks and post offices and cinemas swinging as incessantly, but no more incessantly than usual. But at Newhaven we came suddenly on one of those significant details that make for reality. On a railway crossing was a sentry with fixed bayonet.

It might have been the merest precaution. It might have had no significance at all. If, in fact, the prophecy of the sanguine farmer in the Lewes bar had come about it would doubtless have been merged with other recollections of a tense and trying

week into a series of small signs of crisis. But for me the flash of
the sun on that piece of steel, with holidaymakers shouldering
their way by and the shore a few hundred yards away crowded
with bathers meant the beginning of war.

For the rest of the day I continued to drive the Count about
but I found his enthusiastic planning unendurable. It seemed
that nothing could shake his confidence.

"We'll have a day at Newhaven," he said, "and another at
Seaford. Then we'll work on towards Kent. I'm going to put
out special publicity there this year, on the strength of Martin
Hawkes being a Kentish vicar's son. You'll see. It's been a bad
season, up till now, but we'll pick it up in these last few weeks.
And *next* year . . ."

I felt heartsick and futile, and did not try to make him understand.

On Thursday, when we moved to Lewes, there was another
day so busy and absorbing that once again it was possible to
defy the shadow and look up to the brilliant sun. We took up
our position on the breezy hill, with the town beneath us and
the jail at our side. The *tober* was more than usually crowded
with small boys who fetched water for us and helped to put out
the seating with cheerful gusto, and an Alsatian puppy on the
field played with Dingo, drawing him away from his usual concentration on following my footsteps.

[3]

It was from Lewes that I drove into Hove after lunch to
fetch Bosie Douglas who would see the circus and stay to
dinner at the White Hart. This was the last time I saw him, for
although he wrote often when I was in the army, I did not
return from India until a year after his death in 1945. I described
the occasion in my biography of him* but there is an incon-

* *Bosie: The Story of Lord Alfred Douglas; His Friends and Enemies,* 1963.

sistency between this account and the shorter note I made of his visit in *The Circus Has No Home*, my story of the Rosaires, which makes me realize that my memory for circumstances is not as reliable as I like to suppose. In *Bosie* I describe how I went to lunch with him in Hove and recall our conversation at lunch; in the circus book I say, equally circumstantially, "when lunch was over (a cool August lunch with salad and melon and cream-cheese and coffee in it), I set out with the car to Hove" to bring him back. I think the last must be correct and that I was thinking of another of the lunches I enjoyed with Bosie in Hove. Perhaps it does not matter very much and every detail for the rest of the day is clear.

Bosie's battered felt hat turned up in the front, his heavy boots and shapeless suit were worn with an impatient air as though the prospect of another day had made him hurry over dressing. He was never elegant in dress and this gives away many false claims of acquaintance with him. For some reason it was expected that Wilde's friend even forty years after Wilde's death should have been dressy and blah and so Bosie is often described by those who never knew him. He was a countryman, born and bred in rustic England and in the lowlands of Scotland, and he liked wearing tweeds and strong boots.

He also liked Dingo whom he had met on previous acquaintance and turned to him in the back seat of the Opel.

There was already a large built-up area on the road leaving Brighton for Lewes, almost clear of traffic, and I was speeding along this at forty-five miles an hour when a police-car overtook me. Quite illogically I thought there was something absurd about able-bodied policemen dedicating their time and petrol to booking motorists for exceeding the speed limit in a built-up area while the German Army was on the Polish frontier, but I said nothing and dutifully showed my licence and insurance certificate. But Bosie was angry, not with the police but with me.

"Were you *really* breaking the speed limit?" he asked. "You shouldn't have done that. There was no need to. You should keep to the regulations while I'm with you."

Coming from Bosie who had spent his life defying regulation of most kinds this was amusing. But he soon forgot his irritation.

He enjoyed himself youthfully on the circus field, talking to the Rosaires, making friends with the liberty horses, telling the Count what he had seen at the Cirque d'Hiver a year or two ago. I never calculated his age; he was simply an older man to me as he had been when I had first met him eighteen years before, but I realize now that he must have been sixty-nine at that time and his vitality and gusto were extraordinary. The change I was chiefly aware of in him was a change in his public status, if I may use that overworked and frequently misapplied word. When I had first sat with him in his little study in his mother's house in Draycott Place, hero-worshipping the poet, the rebel, the editor of *Plain English*, it had seemed that he had scarcely a friend in the world and the only man or woman I ever met with him was the soft-spoken Irishman, Herbert Moore Pim, with whom in fact he had quarrelled soon after. He was not yet reconciled with his son and only his mother and sister remained staunchly beside him. This was before imprisonment for criminal libel, and long before he had made his peace with the memory of Wilde, a turning-point in his progress to the tranquillity and charm of his later years. "You surprise me. I wonder they don't erect an equestrian statue," he once said snappishly when I told him that there was no plaque on the house in Tite Street. He was bitter and vengeful. But all that was forgotten now and he had become a sought-after, even revered figure, the centre of pilgrimages to Hove by all who were interested in his hectic life-story, 'taken up' by lovers of the notorious, asked to speak in public—not on 'The Murder of Lord Kitchener and the Truth about the Battle of Jutland and the Jews' in the Memorial Hall in Farringdon Street before an audience of cranks but to the Royal Society of Literature on the Principles of Poetry.

I remember him wandering about the field that day, I think how seldom it was in all the years I knew him that we had met

F

in any surroundings but those of comfortable sitting-rooms or public restaurants. In Belgium we had walked together to the races in Ostend and through the old streets of Bruges, at a house on Shipbourne Hill I had ridden and walked with him and his son Raymond, and once he had stayed with me at Rochester when I had an antiquarian bookshop there, but on the whole we had been together in polite surroundings. Yet he was at his best in the open air.

Above all, he was interested. The circus held no glamour for him but he might have been a journalist intending to write an article on it to judge from the questions he asked and the enthusiasm he showed. No one understood him less, among the inquisitive people who sought him out in his last years, than that pretentious bore Henry Channon who reported that Bosie was entirely wrapped up in his own affairs. Only in literature was this true—his longing for recognition after so many years of hostile indifference was evident. But his attitude to people, to events, to the changing pattern of life, to an experience like this one in unfamiliar country he responded quickly and wholeheartedly.

Not until we were sitting at dinner in the White Hart, eating trout and drinking champagne, did we talk of the war. Bosie, characteristically, had made up his mind about it.

"I don't know why you should think there is going to be a war," he said. "I can tell you there won't be. Last year at the time of the Munich crisis I told my nephew Francis Queensbury the same and if he had listened to me he would have made a lot of money on the Stock Exchange."

So that dismissed the subject. It did not occur to me that I might never see Bosie again. He had been a familiar and beloved character in my life for so long that he was part of it, as my father had been. Even had I known I would not have plied him with last-minute questions about the past for it was the man who had always interested me, the poet and the fighter and not the mere friend of Wilde.

We said good night casually, meaning to meet again next week.

CHAPTER FOURTEEN

War and the Circus

I saw the outbreak of war in terms of a circus closed down before the end of its tenting season and if that seems in retrospect a tangential way of meeting an event of such horrific fatefulness I can only say that this, or something like it, was about as much as most of us could grasp at the time. We are not equipped to compass the events of history except as they affect our own small lives and relationships, and to some fortunate survivor Hiroshima may have meant chiefly the destruction of his milch-cow. Realization did not in any case come to most English people before Dunkirk. I saw it as the end of the pleasant way of life I had been following, but the calamity was more immediate and insistent to the Rosaires who had been so little prepared for it.

After Lewes we went on Friday morning to Newhaven. Our *tober* adjoined a power station which was guarded by soldiers, and a sergeant came over to warn us that the fence between it and us must be regarded with respect, for his sentries had orders to protect it. The town seemed full of soldiers in uniform.

Then the trains began to arrive from London laden with files of summer-clad children who, we were told, were being evacuated to the villages around us. Such an exodus at any other time and in any other circumstances would have appeared to circus people as ordained for their special benefit. Such vast potential audiences brought to the very entrance of our ground! But today the strings of them with their little packets and their unnaturally cheerful teachers only made us look irrelevant and frivolous. People were crowding round the ARP officers with belated inquiries or requests, every telegram desk at the post office had a queue waiting for it, faces everywhere looked taut and anxious, and a passing aeroplane produced a sky-gazing crowd. The public houses were abnormally busy, and their bars, in which there was scarcely room to stand, became silent for each news bulletin.

Among the Rosaires there was some division of counsel. But the Countess remained calmly insistent that they should show that afternoon.

"Whatever happens, there's nothing against that. Even if we have to finish the tour tomorrow."

She was right. That Friday afternoon, less than forty-eight hours before war was declared by Great Britain, they had one of the best houses of the season. I was glad to see Ida riding round as gaily as ever, and Ivor displaying Princess Monice and Vivienne smiling from the trapeze, and Dennis strolling about on his wire, as though this was just one, a normal one, of their performances, as though they would be showing here tonight and tomorrow at Seaford. And I liked to hear the Countess say with a little toss of her head, "We shall go on showing till they stop us, if there are fifty wars on. We've booked this ground haven't we? Well. So long as there are people to come and no law against it, we shall go on!"

But an hour after the afternoon show ended the matter was taken out of her hands. A policeman arrived on the field and quietly explained that as no lights could be shown, and no public performance for a large number of people be given, he must ask them to consider that for the present, at any rate, their show was closed.

[2]

To realize the enormity of that to circus people one must remember the things they themselves had done and endured in their history to prevent it happening, even for a single night. Their tent blown down by a wild gale had been reconstructed somehow, a meagre audience, absence of half the company, a dispute among the tent-men, an animal escaped, an organized attempt to prevent them showing—all these things they had overcome. Their whole lives were based on the axiom that somehow or other, whatever the difficulties, their show must be given. Now a single and polite policeman had calmly said that they must consider themselves closed.

The Countess was for disputing the matter. Their lights, she said, could be shaded in such a way as not to illumine the canvas, and they need show no lights outside the tent. Surely, she argued, their livelihood could not be taken away from them just like *that*. Why, war wasn't even declared yet. But to her, too, the grim truth became too evident for denial. The thing was on us, the tour was ended, the circus was closed.

Nobody showed much excitement. The Count regretted the probable loss of his showing at Seaford, and his months in Kent, but was not altogether convinced even about that.

"It isn't *certain*, yet," he pointed out. "We may be able to finish the tour after all."

The tent-men were at a loss when the time for the evening show approached and there was no whistle, no dynamo started to supply the lighting, no work to do. The great tent stood in darkness, the zoo shut up ready for travelling, our own waggons unfamiliar without the bright squares of orange and red when their lamps were lighted—the whole aspect of the circus field was grim and dreary.

That night the scene in the pub near our *tober* was unforgettable. The room was a large one and it was crowded—soldiers, largely, a good many women, railway workers, sailors and our own crowd, everybody more than naturally good-humoured and chatty, drinking hard, jocular. There was a piano and one of those indefatigable pub pianists who follow the common whim, beating out any tune requested. Soon the whole crowd was singing lustily, tearfully, alcoholically, but

singing in chorus to the tunes he played. These—it was surprising to me—were the popular tunes of the last war—*Keep
the Home Fires Burning, Tipperary, Till the Boys Come Home, If You
Were the Only Girl in the World* and the rest. Where had they been
in retirement? By what instinct for popular emotion did that
pianist remember them now? Malcolm Muggeridge, only a
year later was to perceive this:* "Now old uniforms were
brought out, put away long ago; old songs were remembered,
thought to have been forgotten; old ways were resumed, old
emotions experienced, old hopes revived. No new war was
possible, so an old one would have to suffice." If fighting
had started at once we should have died to the tunes of our
fathers twenty years ago, with no more sense of direction.

[3]

Next morning there was a conference. I have never felt more
assailed by responsibility than when the Rosaires expected
advice from me. It was the last thing I had ever supposed that
I could give, or for which I might be approached by them. The
Rosaires never asked advice. Why indeed should they? Their
equipment for the life they led—the only life they visualized
as possible for them—was complete. Tenting, working, performing, giving pleasure and earning a living, all the arduous
business and checks of their profession—these things they
understood, no one better.

But suddenly another world had overflowed into theirs,
suddenly strange issues had made themselves felt, and for the
first time they were faced with a situation the roots of which
they did not understand. Hitler, Poland, Russia, war. . . . Not
to my circus friends alone among the thousands from whom
sacrifices were to be asked were these names remote and meaningless. But perhaps to them more ironically than to others.

The Thirties, by Malcolm Muggeridge, 1940.

They had asked so little of society; their tribal existence depended so slightly on the political structure; they had no home to defend. Now, with the abrupt closing of their show, it seemed to them that the people of another world, a world of politics and armies, of dictators and democrats, had struck at them.

I, who had to be presumed to know more of that world than they, was expected to tell them succinctly what could be expected of it, as they could have told me in a fews words what would come from *their* sphere in a crisis. Rather grudgingly, perhaps, for they are accustomed to forming their own decisions swiftly and on the data they so amply possess, they demanded of me, "Will it really start? Shall we declare war? Will it last long? Who will be on our side? Who against us?"

They resented the necessity of asking me questions, always having regarded me as an innocent in their world, an ignorant recruit, whatever I might be among householders and such. They resented it even more when I was able, by chance, to provide them with a ground on which they could stand their waggons without payment till they decided what to do, their present ground being hired for large prices to fairs and circuses visiting Newhaven. For this they could not forgive me. That someone so unrelated to the circus by profession, however close his personal ties might be, should put them under an obligation of this kind was unendurable.

The ground was at Smarden, a remote village on the levels of the Weald near which, two years ago, I had rented a house my father had once occupied. Yet more remote, the ground was beyond a lonely pub, the Smarden Bell—'out on the Headcorn–Biddenden road' was its situation as usually stated locally. In *The Happy Highways* I described it "Just after the First World War [Bob Parker] had fallen a victim to one of those plot-of-land swindles which took the gratuities from officers and other ranks alike. A so-called property company had bought for almost nothing a few acres of poor ground near Smarden and spent some money on drawing up an elaborate prospectus

which promised plot-purchasers a new city of shops and indus-
tries. A large-scale map was published showing where 'market',
'church' and 'hotel' would stand, and a public auction disposed
of some hundred 'plots' of bare meadowland a few miles from
a railway or any house or place of business. Every other
purchaser soon realized he had been duped and abandoned
his hopes, but Bob Parker was an obstinate man and undeterred
by finding that his plot was in the middle of a wilderness,
he built himself a wooden shack there and started a smallholding.
As the years passed and the surrounding sites remained barren
he took over more ground and invested in a few sheep. Occasionally, as he used to tell us, one of the original mugs would
arrive to see the state of his investment but he was usually glad
to sell Bob his elaborately drawn up deed for a pound or two
and Bob remained in possession." Now Bob had died in the
previous year and I telegraphed to his widow who worked and
lived in London for permission to use the ground and she
agreed.

We reached it late on Saturday afternoon. I remember that
untidy waste as we found it in the sunset—not a house in sight,
the hedges unkempt and thistles the only growth in any pro-
fusion. The empty sheds and chicken-houses which my old
friend had erected, and the stacks of rubble and timber which
he meant to use, alone showed any sign of human habitation.
Just as the circus should have been opening to a crowded
house in Seaford their waggons began to arrive. It had been a
long drive from Newhaven, and the elephants and horses
would be on the road for two days or more. But all of the circus
that was petrol-driven came, and took up positions on the
lonely fields.

The tent-men tried to crack a joke or two about the *tober*.
"Bet we're packed here," they said. "Where's Jimmy going to
mark out for the tent?" they asked. But their words fell dully
on the silent evening. There was not even, in that lane, a passer-
by to watch the arrival of a circus.

After that, the actual declaration of war on Sunday morning, the sirens moaning (by mistake it was said) as Chamberlain finished broadcasting, were anticlimax.

[4]

I did not take my trailer to join the Rosaires' waggons on their lonely ground but kept it in an orchard near the Bell. Baffled as we all were by the international lull which followed the declaration of war, I yet recognized it quite plainly as the end of my life in London, of being or trying to be someone of consequence, of running down the Edgware Road in the Opel to talk things over with Louis Golding in Hamilton Terrace, of writing feature articles for the *Mirror* or novels for Walter Hutchinson, of entertaining my miscellany of friends and acquaintances, of going abroad on the smallest provocation, of driving about the London streets at night, of all the pleasant things which made these last two years seem so richly eventful.

I had an overpowering fear of being in an air-raid on London, and thus a phobia for London itself. This, like most fear, was the result of a particular imagining. I did not feel safer in the country because the country was less likely to be bombed—nothing so logical. On the contrary it seemed to me that a bomb on my orchard was as probable as a bomb on my London flat. But I saw London aflame, walls collapsing around one, the Thames choked with rubble from the ruins of the city, terrified crowds rushing nowhere, the destruction of Sodom and Gomorrah, leaving scarcely a survivor of all its millions. This was a very real and immediate menace in my mind and it continued to be for nearly eight months till the air bombardment actually began, when I mysteriously forgot all about it.

On the Tuesday I persuaded the husband of Cissie Rosaire, a knife-thrower with a square show of his own who had rallied to the family, to bring two of his waggons to Upper Berkeley Street and strip my flat of its contents which I would store in Tenterden. Derrick Rosaire and three of the tent-men came with us and loaded my furniture as easily as if it were their props and seating, and we came away before dusk. The parents of Myles Eadon, who lived in uneventful retirement in Kent, were startled by the arrival of a circus waggon at their doors to drop off their son's belongings.

A few days later Martin Hawkes the lion-tamer married Ida Rosaire and I attended my third wedding in that year, and certainly the strangest. (I had never been to a wedding before 1939 and have not done so since.) There were few guests in the long aisle of the newish church, with its smell of scrubbed floors and show of ritualism still faintly daring. But what guests there were claimed the attention of passers-by. For there was Little Freddy standing next to me, just able to see over the pew top to where Martin and Ida stood; there was Vivienne, looking cool and lovely against the tall arches of the chancel; there was the Countess; there were Wally and Cissy; while across the aisle in notable contrast were the less spectacular friends of the bridegroom's family a little curious about the circus into which Martin, who had once been intended for the Church, was marrying. Derrick was a sturdy best man, who wore top-boots under his trousers. There was no signing, no nonsense, no confetti, no photographers, no interminable family reunion, no troupe of performing children to clutch the bride's train, no gaping crowd at the church door. We returned to Smarden to celebrate. The tent-men had been busy up on the lonely stretch of land, for behind the Countess's waggon a big table had been built up with seating unloaded from the lorry, and spread with flags, and piled with food and drink. Benches had been arranged round it—flowers had somehow been procured, and a great wedding-cake glittered like snow in the last light of the sunset.

During that week Dennis married Emilia, a Spanish acrobat to whom he had been engaged for some time, and Ivor his Yorkshire girl. They had intended their weddings to take place at 'turning out time', the opening of the tenting season next year, but in the crisis—not so much of world war but of their closed down circus—the tribe was drawn closer together. Then —it cannot have been more than a fortnight after the declaration of war—they all decided to return to their winter quarters at Billericay, abandoning hope of further tenting that year, and their waggons and lorries pulled out of the field to make for Woolwich Ferry. I was left alone.

[5]

How much alone I only realized in the weeks after the last waggons had gone. Never before, and only once since have I felt that kind of isolation. Of my family my eldest brother returned to the RAF in which he had fought in the First World War, while my sister joined the WRAF. One of my younger brothers was already with his Territorial unit in France while the other had joined the RAOC in the first week of war. My mother was kept busy writing to the five of us.

Of my friends I had similiar tidings. Ernst Thoma had written to me a fortnight before saying rather naively that we might not be able to communicate for some years but that 'as soon as it was over' we would be in touch. Robert Cahiza was in the Maginot Line. Myles Eadon, Barton Wills, the young men I had met at the Supercharger Club were all in the services and Michael Harrison and Richard Blake Brown were soon to be.

I slept in my gimcrack trailer with nothing but painted three-ply between me and the elements and tried to orientate myself as the days of the phony war began. Petrol became unobtainable which made me feel even more marooned amongst the fruit trees. Planning was futile but I could not yet decide to abandon myself to fate and the commands of others by going to the nearest recruiting station and enlisting. I waited to see what would happen, convinced that something must.

I felt no self-pity—far from it. I wanted to be alone, with

Dingo, in an orchard in Kent, near a familiar pub, unvexed by responsibilities, unhampered by possessing a home. I felt I was waiting for a summons, not from the army but from some unguessable destiny to which I would gladly respond. In fact, for the next episode.